I'M A WORK-AT-HOME MOMMY—YOU CAN BE TOO!

I'm a Work-at-Home Mommy—You can be too!

A guide for moms who want to work at home.

Teresa Lyons

Writers Club Press

San Jose New York Lincoln Shanghai

I'm a Work-at-Home Mommy—You can be too!
A guide for moms who want to work at home.

Writers Club Press
an imprint of iUniverse, Inc.

For information address:
iUniverse, Inc.
5220 S. 16th St., Suite 200
Lincoln, NE 68512
www.iuniverse.com

ISBN: 0-595-25033-5 (pbk)
ISBN: 0-595-65003-1 (cloth)

Printed in the United States of America

To Jess and Jordon, my two favorite little angels.

You haven't lived your fullest until you've followed your dreams…

—Anonymous

Contents

ACKNOWLEDGMENTS

I would like to thank all the terrific moms I interviewed for my book. You were all great about submitting your input back to me quickly even though you are very busy taking care of your family, your home, running a business-and having fun! God Bless all of you and enjoy your success!

INTRODUCTION
A word from the Author

As I stood there in the restaurant I worked at, I watched the customers file in and out of the place. I wondered what I was doing here. I was one of the managers, worked long hours and barely saw my two young children. I knew there was something else out there for me-something better. I always had the dream of being my own boss. After working another fifteen-hour shift, I decided to do research on working at home. I didn't realize how many opportunities there were out there. (I loved to write and even took classes, but I didn't think I could make a living at it at the time.) So, after searching the Internet and pouring over many books by mothers who started their own businesses, I realized that they pretty much started out the same way as I had and they found their dream. Just as I suppose you are too, or you wouldn't be reading this. Then I thought to myself, wouldn't it have been easier if I had found a book where some clever person had already had everything researched for me? I knew I wanted to help other moms find what they want to do and in the process, I found my true dream-writing.

1

WHAT BUSINESS IS RIGHT FOR YOU?

Now, before I start, I want to tell you how I broke into leaving my secure job and beginning my journey into the work-at-home life. I didn't start out jumping into writing. Though, it was truly what I wanted to do. Actually, what I decided to do (after much research) was to open a daycare. See, I started out thinking that I didn't care what I did, as long as I did it at home so I could be with my kids. This was my big mistake. Don't get me wrong, it's not that I didn't really enjoy it and it can be a great home business. It just wasn't what I was meant to do. But, like I said, I didn't realize how important it was to love what you do. I did daycare for two years, which enabled me to learn a lot about running a business. I found out-sometimes the hard way-how to keep better records, be more firm with people, how to protect your business, etc. I don't regret doing it at all. It was a great learning experience. But, I needed more. My creative side wanted to come out.

Finally, one day I sat down and wrote down every interest I had and what I would want to do if I could do anything. After I finished, there was one thing that seemed to be in every business that I wrote down-writing. So, I decided to take out some of my old writing and looked at a story I had started a year ago. I started writing it again during naptime and playtime and anytime that I had a free moment. (I found myself so looking forward to finding that free minute to write that it almost became obsessive.) There were times that I had to force myself to put my writings away because it was taking time away from my kids.

I still, at this point, didn't think of writing as a career though. It still hadn't dawned on me that I could be doing something I truly loved and make money at it. I just felt that need to write. Anyway, after a couple of months, I finally finished it. I sent it off to be published and sat back and sighed. I was proud of myself at this accomplishment. I went back to running my daycare and all the while, thinking about that book.

Another couple of months later, my book arrived. There it was in big bold print, *The Accident* by T. A. Lyons. Wow! I was excited and numb at the same time. Then, it finally hit me. This is what I want to do. My childhood dream that had always been there, hidden. So, I kept my daycare going (Well, I still needed the income and I didn't want to go broke!) and I explored my writing possibilities at the same time. I knew I liked to write fiction but I also was fascinated with information on the Internet and with other women in my situation that worked at home or wanted to. So, I decided that I would still work on my novels but also get involved with helping other moms accomplish their dreams. After more research, I put together an online magazine called *MommysBiz @Home.* (**www.MommysBizatHome.com**)

I was so excited (once again) about it; I worked on it every chance I could. It was hard for me to believe still that I could have fun making a living. I had finally found my niche.

FINDING YOUR DREAM

After reading my long story about how I got to where I am today, I hope it made you realize that you can't just want to work at home. That can't be your only motivation-though, it can be a big part. You have to find something you like to do or you won't make it. Why? Because YOU are your main motivation to make it succeed. YOU have to be your main cheerleader and if you aren't there cheering yourself on nobody else will. Remember, you are here reading this now because you aren't happy where you are at now. So, you have to be happy where you want to go too. As Diana Ennen of Ennen's Computer Services, suggests, make sure this is the right business for you and you will be more successful if you do.

When is the best time?

There really is no "best time" to start a business. If you want to start something (business) than start it. Don't wait for the timing to be right. If you do, then next thing you know, your kids will be grown and you'll have missed it. Just as everything else in life, if it feels right, than go for it.

Is your present job costing you money?

Decide if your present job is costing you more money to work outside of the home. Take into consideration just how much it costs to go to work and you might find that it's cheaper for you to stay home!

- *Clothing expense*—Depending on where you work, most jobs require you to dress professionally, which can add up fast. This could amount to $100 a month!

- *Transportation*—Wear and tear on your vehicle, car payments and gas usually comes to about $400 a month.

- *Food costs and misc.*—Eating out or convenience food run about 80-90 a month.

- *Childcare*—Childcare costs can be the leading expense to the working parent. This can run around $400 a month just for one child. Not to mention most won't watch them if they are sick. Which could lose you a day's pay for having to stay home.

That total comes to almost a $1000 a month-a lot, isn't it?

Don't forget that it puts you in a higher tax bracket and most of those expenses can't be deducted.

Advantages of working at home:

- *Dress down*-lower clothing expenses.

- *Less use of car*-less gas used and lower maintenance.

- *More cooking at home*—lower food bills and eat healthier.

See how the advantages of working at home have saved you money already?

More reasons to work at home:

- More freedom to be there for your children.

- Your children don't have to be dropped off at the daycare and be raised by someone else.

- You're the boss!

- You can work around your family instead of putting them on the back burner.

- You love what you do!

- You don't have to feel guilty staying home and taking care of your sick child.

Need I say more? The pros are endless. So, if you need reasons to help you or to convince someone else, there are plenty!

One reason, which I want to stress, is, if you want to get rich fast. A successful business takes time and work and maybe some day, you'll be very comfortable, but don't expect to be a millionaire in your first month. There are no easy roads to riches out there. Doing something you love is priceless, remember that first.

Some downfalls of owning your own business.

True, there are lots of reasons why you should start a business, but it's not all peaches and cream. Here are some cons of working for yourself:

• You are the boss-nobody to throw the problems to.

• You may not have a steady paycheck.

• Your business really never goes away. You may be on call.

• All the paper work is up to you. Filing taxes, insurance, business investments.

• Isolation.

These may be a small price to pay for going after your dream.

"How do I start?"

That's easy. Do what I did and sit down and take out a notebook and pen and start listing everything you like to do. It doesn't matter what it is. There seems to be a business for every hobby out there. Once you have that done, take a long hard look at it. Which activities jump out at you? What made you smile more when your wrote it down? Are you a great cook? Think about a certain dish that you get a lot of compliments on? Maybe you could market it. Or, do you like to make things? Crafting is very hot and there is a lot of information out there on how to market it. Do you get where I'm coming from? Find your niche first.

You might still say to yourself, "But, I really don't have any skills."

Wipe that thought from your head. Every woman has skills. Especially mothers. Think about what you already do. Your kids daily activities are in your hands-to chauffeur, cook, clean and get them where they need to go. The upkeep of your house is mainly up to you to make sure it's in order and in working shape. If married, your husband probably relies on you to remind him of important dates, doing some errands, buying that birthday present for your mother-in-law since he keeps forgetting. Looking back over that paragraph, as far as I can tell, you already are running a ton of businesses and you don't even realize it. You are a secretary, chauffeur, handy-man (woman) computer consultant, organizer, party planner, chef, errand service, and even a personal shopper. The sad part is you're not even getting paid for it!

So, double think about your capabilities. Smile when you realize what you are really worth.

Research, research...

Don't start your business until you've done as much research as possible. Read as much as you can on the subject first before you put a dime down on it.

Talk to other people who do the same for a living. Get first hand experience if possible. This can be done through internships, volunteering or working for someone first. If this is already a hobby, then consider market research. This can determine if there is a need for what your business has to offer.

Ask your friends what they would pay or what they wouldn't. Ask what part of your service they would like or want to see available. Tell them to be as honest as possible. You could try out the public and volunteer your services to a charity and see what the results are.

Way to go!

When I was young, I was always dreaming up stories in my head and writing them down in my journal. My stories seemed to be the ones picked for examples for the class; which encouraged me to keep writing. I will always remember my 7th grade teacher, who always encouraged me to write. She would marvel over my creativity and would write rave remarks on my papers about how she always looked forward to my next adventure story. Though, she may have long forgotten me, I will

never forget her and her words of encouragement. They are my inspira-
tion to keep writing when my confidence is down.

Anyone starting their own business needs encouragement and moral
support from whatever source they can get. Unfortunately, this may be
hard to come by. People close to you may not be too encouraging. It's
just how human nature is some times. They don't do it on purpose.
They just want you to play it safe. Do not let that discourage you.
Once they know that you are very serious about doing this, they will
come around. Believe me, I went through my own ordeal. When I
decided to start a business, I had just purchased a new home, had just
got a raise at work and had a safe job. It took my family awhile to
decide to back me up and be okay with my new business.

Don't get me wrong, though. I'm not saying your husband or
friends will not encourage you. I have found that many moms have
loving, supporting husbands. Just don't let it get you down if they
aren't. Find another source for your cheerleader. And don't forget
there's always you to cheer yourself on!

HOW TO AVOID A SCAM

One thing that I need to point out-no, drill into your head-is do not,
under any circumstance, fall for a get-rich-scam. There is a lot out
there too. Crooked businesses know that there is an increasing demand
to work at home these days for mothers and they will prey on you.

On my site, scams are not tolerated. If one slips by us and it is
reported, their ad is taken down immediately. I just can't believe someone would try to crush an innocent mother's dream to be home with
her children. But, the fact is there are people like that out there. We
just need to avoid them. You might have already been scammed at one
time or another—I bet we all have. Unfortunately, I was one of them
too. A long time ago, I sent away for the home assembly product deal.
I'll tell you right now, don't ever do that. You buy their materials and
make products shown in the tiny picture that they send you. Then you

send it off to them with high hopes only to have it sent back not accepted. And I'll tell you; they won't ever accept it. They make money selling their materials-YOUR hard earned money!

WHAT TO LOOK FOR:

- Easy money

- No experience

- Make money while you sleep

- Make $10,000(or whatever huge amount) a day

- Only work a couple hours a week

As the old saying goes, if it sounds too good to be true...

These ads appeal to our greedy side. We all want to be a millionaire and get rich quick. These businesses take that greedy thought and blossom it into thinking it's true. All they are doing is getting your hard-earned money from you so they can be the millionaires. Even if you think, "This one sounds legal." Don't be fooled. It will only lower your self-esteem and take your money that you need for your real business.

Some scams may be hidden well and you might really think it's for real. Before signing up or whatever, do your research. Call the better business bureau in the state the company is in. You can also look at their site: **http://www.bbb.org**.

I also always tell a mom that a real company doesn't ask you for money anyway.

I WANT TO REPORT A SCAM

Let's say you found a scam and want to put them out of business. What should you do? It depends on the scam.

- If it was sent through the mail, call your local Post Office and report the scam.

- You can call the National Fraud Information Center at 1-800-876-7060.

- Call the BBB in their state.

- Call the state attorneys office in your state.

The last advice on scamming is just remember that if you are patient, one day you will be able to enjoy your financial success but until then, reap the rewards of seeing your baby's first steps or waking up each morning knowing you are home and working for yourself. Just be patient and start a real business that in reality, will take some time to get going!

2

WE ALL NEED A PLAN.

Okay, so you know what you want to do, where do you go from there? I suggest a business plan. This will show you on paper what your expenses and what your business will cost to start. A business will fail if you don't have a good business plan. This is your future, so do it right! You will be thankful later. This can also be used as documentation for a potential loan if needed.

HOW DO YOU CREATE A BUSINESS PLAN?

There are many small business counselors available or contact a small business owner and ask them what they did. Or, you use what I did for mine. The questions I came up for myself are as follows:

1. DESCRIBE YOUR BUSINESS-MAKE SURE YOU KNOW EXACTLY WHAT YOUR BUSINESS IS.

   _____

   _____

   _____

2. IS THERE A NEED FOR WHAT I WANT TO DO?

   _____

   _____

   _____

3. LONG TERM GOAL-WILL MY BUSINESS BE IN DEMAND IN 3 TO 5 YEARS?

    _____
    _____
    _____

4. WHAT WILL I USE FOR FUNDING?

    _____
    _____
    _____

5. WILL I NEED A LICENSE?

    _____
    _____
    _____

6. WILL THERE BE ANY ONGOING EDUCATION REQUIRED?

    _____
    _____
    _____

7. WHAT SUPPLIES AND EQUIPMENT FOR THE BUSINESS?

    _____
    _____
    _____

8. INSURANCE REQUIRED?

    _____
    _____
    _____

9. WHAT OTHER COSTS? UTILITIES, ETC.

    _____

_____
_____
_____

10. WHO ARE MY TARGETED CUSTOMERS?

_____
_____
_____

11. HOW WILL YOU REACH YOUR CUSTOMERS?

_____
_____
_____

12. WHAT MARKETING COSTS WILL BE INVOLVED?
    ADS?_____
    WEBSITES?_____
    PUBLICATIONS?_____

13. ANY FREE ADVERTISING?

_____
_____
_____

14. WHAT MAKES MY BUSINESS DIFFERENT FROM COM-
    PETITORS?

_____
_____
_____

15. WHAT ARE MY WORKING HOURS?

_____
_____
_____

16. WHAT IS MY COMPETITION?

_____

_____

_____

17. WILL CUSTOMERS BE COMING TO MY HOUSE?

_____

_____

_____

18. WILL I NEED A ROOM JUST FOR MY BUSINESS?

_____

_____

_____

19. TRANSPORTATION-WILL I NEED TO PURCHASE A VAN OR TRUCK?

_____

_____

_____

20. WHAT DO I NEED TO MAKE ENDS MEET?

_____

_____

_____

What do you need to charge to make a profit?

Here's where women tend to have problems. A big one is guilt. I don't know why, but we tend to not charge what we are worth. Must be a mom thing, I think. When I started my daycare, I charged $80.00 a week per child for full time. I felt bad for the parents working and not being with their child and knowing the cost of living. Well, the guilt factor set in and I was under charging for my services. We did crafts and trips and preschool classes. Those costs were killing me. I finally had to take charge and not feel sorry for them. I was in business to make money and I had to let them know that. I decided to feel sorry for myself instead (well, something like that) and raised my prices to $100 a week. The great part was that the parents were willing pay it! Their kids liked being here and they liked me too and didn't want to lose a good daycare.

You need to charge what you deserve. Don't over do it though. On the other side of the coin, it could hurt you too. Over charge and they won't bite. This may take a little while to come to a sufficient charge for your services or product. But, you'll figure it out.

MONEY

Money, money, money...

You can't start any kind of business without some of it. You wonder how you should finance it? Well, it's not always an easy question to answer. If this is something you plan on starting out full-time, you will also have to plan on having enough money to live off of until your business takes off.

Sure, we would love to be able to open up shop and in the first week, triple our salary. But, sorry to say, that probably won't happen. A successful business takes time.

A loan from the bank.

There are lots of businesses that can be started on a shoestring. I started mine with just a $100. Don't over do it. Start as small as you can and if you can do it without a loan, great. You don't need to jump into debt before you begin. But, if you do need to get a business loan, plan on asking for a lot because most won't deal with anything under $100,000. You may be able to ask for just a personal loan. This may be a secured one. Like I said, don't get in over your head and think this out first.

A woman, who started a computer consultant business out of her home, confesses, "I went all out for my office. I bought a huge expensive desk, fancy supplies and an expensive computer." She felt this would make her look more professional. She had spent a bundle before she even got her first client and racked up high interest. She has been in business for a year now and just now is finally seeing a decline on her balance. She advises, "Don't do what I did. Work your way up to the fancy stuff." She adds, "When you're sure in knowing that your business is where it needs to be, then you can start getting more fancy."

SCORE may be of help in finding a financing source for you. They can help in other ways too. They give great business advice and helpful information pertaining to your specific business. Visit them on the web: **http://www.score.org**.

Borrowing from friends or family

I do not recommend doing this if at all possible. First of all, you may have a hard time convincing them. I feel the pressure would be too much to handle if you did get the loan. Especially if it is for a very large amount. They may try to take over your business knowing their money is at risk. You know, looking over your shoulder. Making sure you don't mess up and lose their money.

Using your own resources

Do you have a credit card? This may be a route you should take. True, the interest rates can be high, but a lot of times you can call your credit card company and ask if they can match another card's lower interest rate. Most will for a limited amount of time, like 6 months. You could possibly have it almost paid off by then, or switch to another card at the same rate.

Should I dip into my savings?

I would recommend this if you set a limit and talk it over with your husband and decide together what your limit will be.

This way of financing has its benefits of not owing anything, but it also leaves you without savings in case of an emergency. You should build it back up as soon as possible as one of your first priorities.

Where should I put my business income/expenses?

You will need to have a separate account for your business to pay business-related expenses and to deposit your earnings. Keep this totally separate from your personal account. This will let you keep better records and take checks written to your business name. It's good to have a credit card that's only used for your business. Even if you're tempted to use your business funds for personal expenses-Don't. If you start doing that and keep doing it, your dream will quickly go down the toilet.

3
AM I LEGAL?

Is this legal?

Okay, let's talk about the topic that everyone hates; taxes. We must all pay them. There is no way around it. So, don't cheat Uncle Sam! He cares whether your business is big or small. Making lots of money or little. I pay mine in four installments a year. This is also why you need very organized books. If you aren't good with books, you may want to hire an accountant. Luckily, my sister is an accountant, so I have her do mine. I'd rather not look up every deduction rule and what not and concentrate on my business instead. But, deductions are good, so take advantage of them! I found out that you could even deduct your cable bill when you run a daycare! Here are some sources on taxes on the net:

http://www.smbiz.com/
http://www.quicken.com/taxes/
http://www.btbtax.com/

WHAT OTHER LEGALITITES MUST YOU PAY ATTENTION TO?

Zoning laws

To save yourself headaches later, please check with your city hall for local zoning regulations. If you don't have heavy traffic coming in and out of your house, you should be fine. This is all really just to make sure you aren't making your neighbors mad. It still is very important because you could be shut down.

Do I need a business license?

Most businesses need some sort of license to conduct business. Contact your city hall to find out what your local state requirements are.

What about my business name?

Please put a lot of thought into this one. As I have found out, by writing, the name of a book is the hook, line and sinker of getting someone to pick it up. So, will be the name of your business. Stick to what it is you do. Don't confuse people by not putting something in your name that relates to your business and tell them what it is that you do or sell. For example, my daycare's name is *Little Angels Daycare*. Had I named it, *A Little Heaven in My Home*, a person may not know what I was offering. There are many cute names a person can come up with, but give your customers a clue as to what you actually do.

Great, now you have a name. Whether you're convinced that nobody has ever thought of the unique business name you came up with, you still have to register it. This is a process of doing business as, or DBA. Pretty much telling the public your fictitious name. Make sure you place an announcement in the paper also. This is all done for a small fee. Like, around $20 or so.

Are you selling a product?

If you are selling something, you will need a state sales tax certificate. This will let you pay the state tax money on your product.

On wholesale items, a resale tax certificate is required. I had thought about making gift baskets at one point and found this out when wanting to purchase a large amount of baskets at wholesale. They are pretty strict on this too. (Wholesalers)

How valuable is my business?

Very-and so are you! A big mistake a business owner can do is not to insure their business with liability insurance. This will protect your business and your personal property. The high cost of this type of insurance does discourage some mothers from starting their business and dream. Do some comparison shopping for the cheapest but make sure it can provide the right service for your needs. Sometimes, your regular insurance company will offer a discount if you carry everything through them, like your car, house and liability. Check around and don't give up. Don't let this step keep you from moving on-and don't think you don't need it. You don't want to lose your house because somebody gets food poisoning from your famous egg salad croissant. There are some decent companies out there-Just shop around first.

Now, what about me?

One of the biggest disadvantages of working for you is losing that taken-for-granted health insurance. All of a sudden, your $50 a paycheck premium jumps to $600 a month! Don't worry, there are cheaper policies. Insurance companies are realizing more and more women are leaving the workforce and starting their own businesses. Some of us are lucky enough to be covered on our spouse's policies but there are single moms out there too. Do your research. Check out organizations of other business you can pay into. If you can't find any in your field, then you'll just have to start hunting. Some companies I've found have reasonable rates.

Insurance is another cost to your business, but yet another step closer to your success.

4

MARKETING

Hey everybody! I exist!

Okay, you got everything together and now you are ready to be seen, be heard, and make money! Only thing is nobody knows you are out there. Wouldn't it be great if you could just put a sign on your front door that says, YES, WE ARE OPEN! Just doesn't work that way. You'll have to advertise your business. The rough part of starting your own business-especially from home where nobody can see your office. That is why this will be one of the longest chapters in the book and most valuable source for your business to succeed.

Sure, you've got it all worked out. You're telling your friends and family-which is great, and I hold word-of-mouth as your most valuable marketing tool. But, there are a whole lot of other markets that you can and will need to explore first to get your name out there.

Since I've already mentioned the word-of-mouth resource, I will start there. First of all, you need to make sure your number one sales person has a lot of self-confidence in themselves-that's you, by the way!

Build yourself up!

Praise yourself! You've just started your own business! Be proud and excited. Share this with others and tell them to spread the word. Make sure you find your targeted customers. No matter how great your gourmet dog treats are, a cat lover isn't going to care.

Practice, practice, and practice...

Know your business well. Practice your sales pitch in front of your husband, friends and family. Practice in a mirror, tape your voice and play it back, video tape yourself and make corrections until you've got it down packed.

Find your Niche Market.

What is a niche market? A niche market is a narrowly defined group. This includes the following requirements:

- Everyone has the same interest and needs.

- They want what you can offer.

- You have a compelling reason why they would want to come to you instead.

- The group is large enough to get the business you need.

You must narrow your market as low as you can to cater to the specific interests of the people in that market. Lynn Berthaut, of *A Bunnies Dream*, joined several web rings and posted to several group websites to find her niche market.

Most business owners recognize their targeted market. If you are one who hasn't quite figured it out, you need to evaluate your existing customers you have. For example, if you sold health products, you might find most of your customers are in the health field. You could market to health-related sites or facilities.

Mails here!

Direct mail is one way to advertise though this could make for a costly expense if you go over board. A simple postcard will do. Don't expect most sales from this source. About three percent response is a good return in the mail marketing. That's not very much, but could help.

Flyers

If you have a computer (this should be a must to have if you own a business) design a flyer and go to your local print shop and make a couple of hundred copies. Get the kids together and put wherever businesses will let you.

Hey, buddy! Got a business card?

These are a must. They go with you everywhere and a quick way to land a new client. I first started out without any business cards and I thought, if I had a dollar for every time someone asked me for one…

You can design them yourself if you would like, using your own computer. There are many programs available out there. Or, you can design them online and even get free ones. I designed my first batch from this place:

http://www.vistaprint.com/

Give them to your friends and family too and ask them to pass them out.

Networking

I just recently found a new inexpensive source for advertising. Networking groups are becoming very popular. What you do is send other moms your flyers and brochures and they send you theirs and you put together packets and hand them out. You can make them more fancy by having samples put with and offer them to your customers as a little thank-you gift.

Can you write?

Newspapers are a big advertising industry. Magazines too. They can be costly and even though I recommend checking into putting in an ad, there are other ways to use them to help you. Could you put together a short article relating to your business that explains enough about it and is interesting?

Contact a publication about your topic interest and they probably will be happy to let you submit it. Don't have that knack for writing? No problem. Hiring someone to ghost write it will be well worth it.

Hey! Have you heard the news?

I send out a weekly newsletter to my subscribers of *MommysBiz @Home* online magazine. These inform mothers about new topics added and other information relating to my magazine like job offers, business ideas, etc. Putting together a newsletter about the field you are in will impress your customers and earn their trust. Send them to your regulars and to potential customers. If you are still nervous, don't fret, if you are running a business, you've got plenty to talk about!

Hot off the Press!

Have you ever heard of a press release? Before venturing off into the business world, I did not know about press releases and how much they can help your business get known. They look just like a news story and you can send them everywhere.

Try your local paper first-especially if you offer a service. If you sell over the Internet, send to national publications. If you've written a book or have a hot new product, hit the talk shows. I think shows geared towards women would be your best option. Who know, maybe this time next year, you'll be talking to Oprah! (Wait, that's MY dream!) Anyway, if you want to know what you should include in your press release kit, I have a few pointers:

- Any awards you have won lately.

- Include tapes of any local radio shows or TV shows

- Anything that can make you sound news worthy

It's okay if you haven't achieved any of that yet. You can always add more to your kit. And yes, you don't just send out one and stop there.

Anytime you want to boast about something to do with your business, go for it.

What does a good press release kit look like?

You will want to look as professional as possible. Use your personal letterhead with your business name on it. Make sure you are sending it to the right editor-no misspellings, please. Include a photo and make sure you don't make your story too long and on the other hand, don't make it too short either.

Interesting, verrrry interesting...

Hold the public's attention with your press release.

Include these items also:

- A business card

- An advertisement(brochure, flyer)

- Comments from happy customers

- Write a book? Send it!

- Tell about yourself

- Where your next signing, speech or event will be.

This sounds like a lot to send and you may think it will be too overwhelming for the editors, but in reality, it will show that you've gotten out there and made something of your business and self and working with the community. They will want to be the first to recognize you and get the publicity before someone else tries to "steal" you away!

Day and night...

Never stop marketing. Do some kind of marketing each day. Toot your horn about your business whenever possible. Cindy Clark, Building Blocks Family Daycare, recommends getting merchandise made up with your business name or logo on it. This is a great way to take your advertising with you wherever you go.

The Common Ad

Find an inexpensive publication that best suits your targeted audience. For example, if you offer a service for senior citizens. Let's say you offer group tours for senior citizens and you know there is a newspaper for the 60+ crowd. Advertise there and spend what you need to but don't go into debt over it.

You've got a friend.

This is tough to do, but don't be shy, ask your regulars if they can refer friends. Offer a discount on your service or product if their friends use you or buy from you. This worked great for my daycare business and present business too. Your customers love the discount and you get more customers. It's a win-win situation.

Build a website and they will come.

The Internet is a great source for advertising. Design a website (or hire someone) Maybe this is already how you run your business. Then you know that banners, free classified ads, news groups and other women's work-at-home sites can help spread the word. Here are some sites that have helped me—and mine of course.

http://www.MommysBizatHome.com
http://www.wahm.com
http://www.mommyco.com

Who's calling?

Don't forget your handy phone book. If you have a business line, you can be listed in the yellow pages. I was called on being listed when the new book was coming out. The price was $300 for the year.

Sample the pot...

I love getting samples. On Saturday afternoons, one special grocery store in our area gives out samples of their specials of the day. I watch how it does help sell their products. The customers get to sample the product, enjoy it and put it in their carts and off they go. Great concept and yes, you can afford it. Hand out your product to a potential big client. You will see a rise in your sales, trust me. A candle consultant took advantage of the Easter season by putting some tealight candles with her business card in plastic eggs and put them in a basket and just started handing them to people at her local mall. She saw a difference in her sales just by doing that. Be bold and don't be afraid to approach people or ask a business if you can set up a temporary table. After all, you're giving them something free, how can they turn that down?

Use Testimonials

Use these on ads, your website, press releases and when ever you talk about your business.

How about a service business?

You may not have a product sample to give away if you offer a service. How about volunteering for a charity service? Offer to do their special awards, dinner or decorate the place if your business provides these services. Be creative!

Don't forget your regulars!

These are the bread and butter of your business. Follow up with them. Send a note of thanks. If possible, send them a sample, coupon, etc. to help bring them back again. This will also let them know how much you appreciate their business.

Get out in your community.

Join any and all organizations you can that deal with your type of business. Make sure you don't forget to go to the meetings. Let them know you exist!

5

HELP! MY HAIR IS FALLING OUT! (OR, AM I JUST PULLING IT OUT?)

Okay, nobody said it would be easy. "A mom" is a job in itself. Actually, you are running two businesses-isn't that a scary thought?

You started all of this because you wanted to be with your kids more, spend time with your spouse, have a clean house. Now, you can't remember what color you carpet is because you haven't been able to find it for weeks under all the mess, your youngest keeps asking, "Daddy, when did Mommy move out?" Finally, you wonder, just when exactly did your husband grow that beard?

Relax, you can get it all under control. You've been excited and even obsessed with your new business-your baby, sort of speaking. So, without realizing it, it's taken over your world. That's normal. You just have to learn how to take a step back once in awhile and get a balance going.

Business vs. Family

No, it's not a fist fight. Don't make your business the enemy of your family. You may be up to your earlobes in deadlines and feel you must put them first over everything, but you can't. You have to learn that there is a time of the day that is strictly used to conduct your business and a time for you personal life-and stick to your guns! Sherry Lochner, a direct sales mom (**www.heavenlysweets.com**) states, "My husband helps me out a lot. He takes the kids off fishing, while I finish up orders. When he isn't home, I fill orders during naps or even at night when the kids go to bed."

I understand that there will be times that business will interfere with family time—a customer has a problem with a logo you've designed and their website business is due to go up in 24 hours. Emergencies will happen. Or your daughter's school is having a mother-daughter breakfast. Make exceptions for that sort of stuff. But, learn to say, "I'm closed for the day." No matter how tempting that added project is.

Now, how did that diaper get in the printer?

Believe it or not, your kids can be of help to you and it can be to an advantage to both of you.

Older kids love to help when it's fun. Let them put stamps on letters or stamping memos. Make a game of it and play post office or see who can stack the most letters. Young children will like to play office too. Get a desk their size and let them have their own "office supplies". Teach them your skills if possible. Show them what it's like to be your own boss. Then they know that they have a choice when they grow up whether to be their own boss or not. It really can teach responsibility—oh, and pay them too!

This will give you the opportunity to mix business with pleasure and also help keep your sanity!

Hear Ye! Hear Ye!

Hold weekly meetings with your family. Catch up with what's been going on in everyone's life. Compare schedules to make sure nobody has something going on at the same time. These "meetings" can be fun at the same time. Go out to eat for the meetings or plan a fun event afterwards. This will entice everyone to be there. Have everyone think up an idea or event they might like the family to do and of course, any problems anyone might have. Make your little ones feel important too.

Hear their ideas also. Make sure you keep this schedule going and don't get away from it-stay organized!

Should I lock my kids up when a client comes over? (Kidding!)

Wouldn't it be a dream to be able to build an office in your backyard? Unfortunately, most of us moms don't have the resources to do that. So, we need to handle this the best way we can. Just be honest to your clients and explain that this is your home besides your business. By all means, you will need to explain this also to your kids and that they need to go color, play quietly in their rooms, or maybe put in videotape while your clients are there. You will come across people that just don't understand and think that children should not be around. Most will understand, though, so don't worry about it.

Housework...

Let your family help in running your business by having them help with taking care of the house. Don't feel guilty in adding a chore or two into their list of regular responsibilities.

This will teach them responsibility and let them know that this will help free up time for more family time.

"Mom, is it McDonalds again?"

Cindy Clark, of *Building Blocks Family Daycare*, has put together an ebook entitled "*Freezer Cooking for Daycare Providers.*" This is intended for daycare providers to help them in planning meals using your freezer, but could work for families also. Plan your meals ahead of time and take advantage of fixing ahead and freezing them.

One woman business owner states, "I kept just fixing the same basic meals each week because it was easy. My husband finally got tired of it and started volunteering to cook twice a week, just so we could have something different. Without him knowing it, he saved me tons of time and hassle and I like the surprise of getting something different every week!"

For more ideas, visit:
http://www.30daygourmet.com

Me, myself, and I...

Amidst all the responsibilities a mom has, between taking care of her family and a business, lies a woman who deserves to be pampered. Don't forget about YOU! Take some special time for yourself. Go to the mall by yourself or take a quiet walk. Lock the door and light some candles and soak in a tub full of inviting bubbles. Savor the moment and relax. Forget about deadlines and school plays or what's for dinner. Take that break you deserve and take one whenever you feel the desire to do so.

"MOM! I went poo-poo again!"

This goes along with business calls too. You may have more flexibility with your phone calls then with clients in your home. These can be done during naptime and/or you will be able to walk away from the noise and close the door if you have to. I would like to add, don't feel bad to "bribe" your child to stay quiet during a contact with a client. Add a lot of praise at how good they were afterwards when you were on the phone.

Coffee break? What's that?

Remember when you were working at your old company and you could savor those two 20 minute breaks and that hour lunch? Just because you're the boss, doesn't mean that you aren't entitled to that. Take a morning and afternoon break (schedule these times in you're appointment book) every day. Even if you can't take a full hour lunch-I do recommend trying to keep it an hour-at least do a half an hour one. Taking a breather will do you good for your business. This gives you a chance to refresh yourself-Okay, your brain. This is also a great time to give your kids attention. Not that you aren't already. I mean, come on, what three-year-old can take care of them self? But, at least it's your undivided attention. Make it special and go to the park for a picnic.

I have found out that there are a lot of moms that love the early morning hours. Get up before everyone else and get as much done as you can. This is also a good time because you are fresh and it's quiet and you really can accomplish a lot.

An apple a day keeps your business running?

I'm sure in all the commotion, that you can still keep your kids in tip top shape by making sure they eat right, get plenty of sleep and exercise. But, are you taking care of YOURSELF too?

Stress can effect your health and wear you out-Fast. Pay attention to your body and what it's trying to tell you. If you are feeling tired, take a nap. If you get hungry, then eat!

Speaking of eating, eating right can help you to stay balanced better. Find a diet that's right for you-and stick to it! Especially breakfast-don't skip it! A busy day can get the best of you and before you realize it, it's dinnertime and you haven't eaten all day. Okay, you might lose that ten pounds that you've been wanting to, but this is not the healthy way and it will show in your work. You need to eat healthy and don't skip a meal. Even if you don't eat very much, get something in your stomach.

Recently, several health related magazines and TV shows have been stating that calcium is a great source for good health. It reduces body fat better and of course we need it for healthy bones. Add fruit and vegetables also to your diet. As we all know, they are a great source of the vitamins we need to stay alert and healthy. After all, how can you run a business sick?

One sheep, two sheep, three sheep...

I know that when you take on the role of a mother, you surrender a decent night's sleep until they are eighteen. But that doesn't mean you need to suffer during your working hours. Take a nap for one of your day breaks if possible and don't feel guilty about it. If your little one goes down for a nap set your alarm for a 30-minute nap and go down too. (This is if you don't have any phone calls to make)

Twenty push-ups a day?

Exercise is as important as eating right. Get out of that chair and move around. It will help your body get circulating again and you will feel better. Get a good exercise tape and make it part of your routine every day. I start out my day with mine. It helps get me going and makes me feel refreshed.

Do you Yoga?

Many people-*even famous people*—swear by this. Annette, a professional errand runner, gets up early every day and practices her yoga. Preferably outside if possible. "It lowers my blood pressure and helps me sleep at night if I do it before I go to bed after a very stressful day."

Even if you can get a half and hour walk in, go for it. I recommend anything you can do outdoors you should. The fresh air is good for you and you get a chance to get out in the public and see other adults. (A gym would be good for this too-only if it fits in with your budget)

Which brings me to my next topic:

ADULT SEPARATION ANXIETY

I loved being able to play games and making crafts with the daycare kids and being able to play with my kids as well, but I also missed communicating with other adults. I did get to talk to the other parents when they picked up or dropped off their kids, but it was a hurried conversation and not very productive to me. It made me sad, because I was single, so I didn't have a husband that was coming home at 5 to fill me in on all the gory details of the adult world.

Some moms get lucky and have adult contact because it deals with their work or service. But, if you strictly deal at home, without the any adult contact during the day, don't let it get you down. Many businesses have organizations that pertain to your line of work. This gives you a chance to socialize and even be able to get advice on your business at the same time. There are mom support groups out there too. I belonged to a Child Care Association that had a meeting every month. I also might drop by a writer's club meeting at my local Barnes & Noble at the mall. Don't forget your friends either. Once they've gotten used to you working at home they will come around. Plan an afternoon together and talk girl talk.

A trip to the Bahamas

Yes, you are allowed a vacation even if you work for yourself. You don't have to go far away, just go some to relax for awhile. I suggest one in the summer and one in the winter. In fact, when I was interviewing moms for my book, a couple of them were taking their vacations at the time, so I had to wait until they got back. Moms are giving themselves breaks, so don't feel guilty to take one also!

What if this business just isn't working?

Don't be discouraged if you've picked the wrong business. Many successful business owners didn't start out doing what they are now. Don't throw the towel in if what you've attempted didn't work. Sometimes, we get steered in the wrong direction. Sometimes, we get caught in a scam. It happens. Don't pull your hair out over this. Set a limit of time and/or money and if it doesn't get going after that, try a different business. Just make sure that you follow the same steps for your next business attempt.

6
SUCCESSFUL MOMS

In all my research, I've found out that there are a lot of successful moms out there. Here are moms, just like you, that wanted something very badly and decided to go for it! Learn how they did it and their advice to you.

BUSINESS SUCCESS COACH

Name: Julie D. Raque
Business: Business Success Coach
Website: **http://www.matrixcoachingservices.com**

In Julie's business, she coaches other widows/widowers who are ready to get their life back on track and add some quality to it. She also coaches others who either want a home-biz or have an existing one and need help with it.

Why did Julie start her business?

I started my coaching business due to the demand. I'm a young widow with kids and other young widows were coming to me for help. Then other women who wanted to run a home-biz wanted my help with that too. So I decided to coach individuals in these two areas.

Are there any requirements for this kind of business?

Personal experience. There are certifications that can be obtained, but they are not legally required.

Any Start-up costs?

Roughly $1000 or less. This includes memberships to 2 coaching communities, website and advertising.

What are your rates?

$250 per month = three 45 minute phone calls with unlimited email support.

How do you market your business?

I place advertisements in different online newsletters. Word-of-mouth and referrals.

Will you ever expand?

Yes. There will come a day when I plan on publishing my book, doing a book tour and having other coaching partners.

Do you have any tips for other mothers?

You have to have a compelling goal. There will be speed bumps along the way that will slow you down, and possibly derail you. If you're goal isn't important enough to you, those speed bumps can cause you to give up. Its HAS to be extremely important to you. And the only 2 things that REALLY stand in your way are fear and doubt. Fear of the challenge that comes your way and doubt if you can get through them.

How do you balance your kids and your business?

My kids are in school. During the school year, the school hours are my work hours. During the summer, we have a set of rules that we live by. No exceptions. I have designated work hours and they find ways to be entertained while I'm working. Sometimes I'll put them to work in my office. This helps. Other times I have family and friends take them for a few hours.

How about your spouse?

Currently single, but dating. Hopefully he'll be my spouse soon. He's self-employed too. So our workdays are flexible.

What is your biggest challenge?

Not giving up. Quitting and going back to a 9-5 job would be easy in times of trouble. But I know I wouldn't be happy and life would be miserable.

Any rewards for doing this?

Having the flexibility to schedule your own hours and your own days. Not having to answer to a boss. Being home when your kids need you. Doing something you LOVE and getting paid for it.

Any other advice for mothers?

Anything is possible. You just have to want it bad enough!

Julie's contact information:

Matrix Coaching Services.

http://www.matrixcoachingservices.com
Julie D. Raque
Business Success Coach
matrixcoachraque@aol.com

"Take a look at your life and ask yourself one question. If you had hired a life manager to manage your life, would you give that person a raise...? Or fire them? If you'd fire them, then you need Matrix Coaching Services! Email me today for your free coaching session!"

GRAPHIC DESIGNER

Name: Colleen Bouchard
Business: Cool Baby Graphics
Website: **http://www.coolbabygraphics.com**

Colleen's business currently has two functions. She designs custom logos, illustrations and websites for people across the country as well as retail and wholesale a CD of electronic clipart. The clipart is a brand new venture that is allowing her to market her designs on a broader scale. Clipart is much more affordable than custom work so she is able to reach many more people, which, she says is exciting.

Why did Colleen start her business?

Cool Baby Graphics started as all great passions do, as a hobby. In 1996 I created a website for my cat Molly. I taught myself HTML (Hyper-Text Mark-Up Language) from books and tutorials. I then started playing around with Graphic software programs-creating my own digital art. I have always been very critical of anything I have done so, I personally, didn't think that the website and graphics were all that great. That is why I was shocked when I received an email from the NY Times—they were interested in interviewing me for an article regarding the new "Homepage Epidemic" that was happening online. They had commented to me that the graphic design was fresh and exciting (not to mention that Molly the Cat was a real stunner!) That positive feedback and the feedback that I received from the site's visitors encouraged me greatly. I slowly started to think that I might have a talent for this line of work. To be paid to do something that I truly loved to do… how great was that! So I slowly built up my confidence and my skills and a following of people that wanted more and more graphics and in 1999 I was ready to launch Cool Baby Graphics.

Are there any requirements for this kind of business?

I always tell my five-year-old daughter when she gets frustrated at learning something new, that everything takes practice-lots and lots of practice. Find something that you want to do and try very, very hard at it. I would have to say that would be the biggest requirement for success. You also need to have patience and you need to be able to take criticism—both positive and negative, you need to be able to ask for help. You also need to lighten up and not take it so seriously all the time.

As far as professional qualifications-it all depends. If you have the time and money to pursue academic training, then go for it. I have a BA in Communication not Graphic Design. I didn't realize that I wanted to be a graphic designer until after college was over. I have attended a few classes that are software specific but overall, I have taught myself everything on my own through books and trial and error. I truly feel that a positive attitude, believe in yourself and perseverance are the best qualifications you could have.

Any Start-up costs?

They were minimal but there were some costs involved. I work from home so a big expense is spared by not needing to rent or lease office space. Not to mention all the other expenses of working outside of the home (gas, food, daycare, wear and tear on the car, dry cleaning, etc.) Plus, everything that I purchase for my business is tax deductible. A great incentive to having a home based business.

The essentials that I needed to begin were a computer, printer, fax machine, scanner, and graphics tablet. I also invested in several different software programs. With my new venture of creating a retail clipart CD, I needed to pay for the CD manufacturing, the booklet printing and the packaging. These are not really huge expenses, but all necessary to do the job.

What are your rates?

Rates change with the market, time and skills. My custom rates are very competitive and even more affordable than many of my competition prices. When it comes to artwork, many people find an artist whose style they like

How do you market your business?

In the past, I have not marketed myself at all. I have never done paid advertising online or off. I was lucky enough to be listed with Yahoo back in the day when it was a free service, and I was lucky enough to have my website rank high on their list. I also have done some free link exchanges with other websites that would have access to my target market. Much of the business that I receive is from word of mouth and by people browsing my portfolio of work. It also doesn't hurt that my services are affordable. With the end result, a product that is of high quality and that I pride myself on providing excellent customer service.

Now that the clipart CD is being released and I am going to be targeting traditional brick and mortar stores, online stores and people that visit Cool Baby Graphics, I am creating a marketing plan. In the next few months, I will be advertising in several scrapbook magazines and sending out media kits to all interested parties. It's a new hat that I will be wearing but one that is definitely necessary if I want this to be a success.

Will you ever expand?

I definitely hope to. My future goals are to do less custom individual work and to concentrate more on mass-produced artwork.

Do you have any tips for other mothers?

Hopefully, you're all blessed with little angels that let you work when you need to.

How do you balance your kids and your business?

Currently I have a 5 1/2 year old and one due September of 2002. It's much easier to walk out the door and leave to go to a job every morning but the psychological affects of doing that with small children can be overwhelming and it's not something I would want to do. I am lucky to have a child who understands and respects my work time. She knows that we are able to spend so much more quality time together by me being at home. We tend to trade off on time a lot. If she lets me have 2 or 3 hours to do work, then I can take her to the park or pool for an hour or so. It's an arrangement that we both love.

How about your spouse?

My husband Steven is wonderful. He is supportive of me and believes in me. The best part of all, he encourages me. He tells me all the time what a great job I am doing and he takes a genuine interest in the business by giving me feedback, ideas, assistance and time to work. I probably wouldn't be able to pursue a home based business without his support and, ahhh… insurance benefits.

What is your biggest challenge?

The biggest challenge for me is time management. You definitely need to be very discipline to work from home. You are so easily pulled in many directions all the time and it can sometimes be difficult to focus on what you need to do. There are always distractions and many times, other people don't understand that working from home doesn't mean that you can just drop everything to go to the mall. You need to stay committed and set a daily agenda for yourself-and learn to stick to it.

Any rewards for doing this?

The rewards are immense. First and foremost, I am able to be there for my daughter. I am not missing out on her growing up and I am actively involved with her every day routine. That is the biggest and best reward.

I am so blessed that I have found something that I really love to do and that I am making a living at it. It's all on my terms and I control the direction I am headed in. There's nothing more empowering.

Colleen's contact information:

Cool Baby Graphics
Colleen Bouchard
Moseley, VA 23120
1-804-639-4338
colleen@coolbabygraphics.com

KIDS PACKAGES

Name: Christine Nicholls
Business: Creative Kids at Home
Website: **http://www.creativekidsathome.com**

In Christine's business, she sends welcome letters, birthday cards, gift announcement, birthday surprise, and craft packages to kids.

Why did Christine start her business?

After university, I worked for a consulting company designing a large relational database to analyze health statistics. I went on to complete an executive MBA program while working full time. It was fun, but it does take over your life for a couple of years. My daughter was born about a year later. She didn't adjust to daycare (infant center right in my office building), was constantly sick, and I was only in the office about 3 days a week. Even with working from home the other two days a week, something had to change. My office was in the midst of downsizing, so I volunteered to take a package and stay home full time.

I was interested in starting a home business, but not sure what business to select. My personal goals had changed to a focus on family while the kids are young, but I wasn't ready to put all my skills and education on the shelf for 5-10 years. What I wanted was a business that would be family friendly and could grow as my time increased.

I investigated a few different home business options, but none of them seemed like the right fit. It was very frustrating to realize how challenging it can be to combine professional work and raising a family. I would find an idea, develop a business plan, only to realize that it would not fit with my goals.

Three potentially successful business plans went back in the file cabinet. Each business idea I investigated didn't meet the goals I had set out. Most businesses are designed by adults who don't spend much time with kids. Even the party businesses (Usbourne books and Tupperware) require you to be out 2-3 nights a week to be successful. It was very frustrating, yet I knew that other women had successful combined home businesses and young children. Fortunately, I happened to hear another woman speaking about how she developed her own business from scratch. She noticed a need in her own family, and figured out how to turn it into a business. The next day, my daughter received a package from her grandmother in the mail. It didn't matter what was in the package, just that she had received mail with her own name on it. I put the two together and started working on the idea that grew into Creative Kids at Home.

Are there any requirements for this kind of business?

There are no formal qualifications required. However, there are many different types of experience that would be useful (running a small business, accounting, Internet marketing, web design, writer, graphics artist, production line, receptionist.). Like most small business owners, I'm learning as I go.

Any Start-up costs?

The costs were much higher than they could have been. Three years ago, there weren't as many choices for who could register domain names, and what shopping carts could be used with a merchant account. The total cost was under $500 not counting employee time.

What are your rates?

A one-year gift subscription includes six craft packages with supplies and instructions for $26.99 US.

What services do you offer?

Welcome letter, birthday card, gift announcement, birthday surprise, and craft packages.

How do you market your business?

a. Free publicity—sending press releases to magazines. We were featured as the 'product of the month' in a Canadian Parenting magazine in November 2000. That single write-up accounted for the majority of our business in that Christmas. We are still getting orders from parents who look at back issues. I continue to send press releases and articles to magazines (on and off-line), but nothing has equaled the impact of that first write-up. These projects take less than 10 hours 2-3 times a year.

b. Search Engine Rankings—optimizing pages to improve our placements in the major search engines. Our site has over 50 pages; so it takes a significant amount of time to plan keyword strategies, implement changes, and then monitor the results after search engine updates. I have contracted help to work on some of our key pages, but then I work some of the changes into other pages throughout the site. I spend about 15 hours a month working on these types of projects.

c. Writing articles—for ezines and off-line publications. Most of the articles are related to parenting so that they will appeal to our target market. Some of the articles are related to issues of running a small business. About 2-3 hours per month.

d. Responding to requests. Many sites are interested in profiling businesses, new products, or people on the web. I try to spend 3-4 hours per week surfing sites for parents and volunteering or applying to be featured.

e. MomPacks, WAHM hits—parents working together to promote each other's businesses. MomPacks are sent out with orders from a variety of 'mom-owned' businesses and contain the promotional materials from other businesses.

I would like to include paid advertising in this list, but it just doesn't account for a large portion of our sales. I am making deliberate choices this year to spend money on some of these strategies since they appear to be the ones that get results (i.e. sales!).

Will you ever expand?

Our business is designed for growth, but not to expand and take more of my time. There are a variety of functions that will be contracted out as our subscription business grows.

Do you have any tips for other mothers?

Find something you can believe in. Make sure it will be compatible with your family's needs (e.g. if your baby wants Mommy to put her to bed, don't go into a party business that has you out of the home 3 nights a week at bedtime).

Check that the business can be profitable with the amount of time you can realistically spend working on it.

Find out what your family is willing to give up to let you pursue your dream (Will your husband make dinner and clean the kitchen 3 nights a week, or will you have to squeeze your business in after 10 p.m.?).

Think about how your kids can help. Younger kids will want to be involved. If your work requires impeccable standards, dangerous chemicals, or breakable objects, then make sure the kids are elsewhere for hours (or have their own project to work on beside you). My business has lots of stuff the kids can help with (counting craft supplies, sticking on stamps...). Even older kids might want to earn some money by helping with your business. It can be a great learning experience and lots of help.

How do you balance your kids and your business?

Some days better than others! Always have a couple of backup plans and a few teenagers who can come and play with young kids after school.

Most days work fine for us. I check my email early in the morning, and process any new orders. By the time the kids are finished breakfast, I try to be finished with my computer time. Most days, we do kid stuff throughout the day. Some days, it includes 'working' on new craft projects or testing ideas for our free library of kid's activities.

Develop a back-up plan for when your kids or you are sick for a week. What happens to your business?

I fit my business errands in around our daily activities. The post office is beside the grocery store. The print shop is on the way to the home of my daughter's friend.

I will let the kids watch ONE TV show if I need to check online and they seem too tired to play. Some times they need a bit of down time too. Even if I were willing to let the kids watch TV all day, they would end up fighting pretty quickly. Kids want to be doing, not just sitting around and it is much healthier for them. Think about how your business can be run by a mom of active kids. Even if your child is 3 months old now, within a year, you'll be chasing after a toddler.

Recently, I switched to a laptop computer. I can take it outside and watch while the kids are playing in the yard.

Have a few special boxes prepared for emergencies. One box could have "office supplies" for the kids to play office. Another could have some yard sale toys that they haven't seen before. A third could have some new books. Anything, as long as it is new and will distract them long enough for you to finish what you need to.

There is no single answer to the question. Just lots of different approaches depending on how the kids feel, what work needs to be done, and what activities are planned for that day.

How about your spouse?

Again, some days are better than others. Usually I try to have dinner ready when he gets home so that we can all sit down together. Often he takes the kids outside and lets me clean up or work depending on what needs to get done the most.

We try to get some time together once the kids are in bed. Now that the kids are getting older, it is easier to hire a sitter so that we can go out for the evening.

When the kids were younger, we just took them with us. It was still nice to get out for dinner, or an evening walk.

What is your biggest challenge?

Marketing. You can spend a lot of money and/or a lot of time without getting any results. I try to track both time and money to focus our resources where we get results.

Any rewards for doing this?

1.   Hearing about how much the kids love the craft packages.

2.   Realizing that my own kids had fun as part of my business. The day we tested rocket launchers was a lot of fun.

3.   Hearing my daughter talk about "our" business.

4.   Realizing that I have developed a successful venture.

Any other advice for mothers?

Keep looking for ideas until you are sure you've found the one that is right for you. If you ever realize that a business is just the wrong fit, give it up quickly even if you have invested lots of time or money. Your family is too important to make everyone miserable over something that will never work. Plan for the future. What will be happening in 3-5 years in your business and how will that fit your personal life? Most Moms can safely design a business that will take more time in the future as the kids get older (unless you are planning lots of kids!).

Christine's contact information:

Creative Kids at Home
http://www.creativekidsathome.com
877-853-6788

HOMEOWNER REFERRAL BUSINESS

Name: Debra M. Cohen
Business: Home Remedies of NY, Inc.™
Homeowner Referral Network (HRN) Business
Website: **http://www.homereferralbiz.com**

In Debra's business, she refers clients (homeowners) to skilled and screened contractors for home repair and services.

Why did Debra start her business?

I launched my business 3 years ago after leaving a full time career for full time motherhood. I had been home for a few months with my newborn daughter and realized that I missed the stimulation of a career not to mention the income.

The idea for a Homeowner Referral Network (also referred to as an HRN) was born out of personal necessity. My husband and I had just purchased our first home and were faced with a challenge all too familiar to homeowners today—where to find reliable home improvement contractors. I realized that there was a need for a service where homeowners could call and find pre screened skilled professionals. My HRN represents a network of contractors. I refer them to clients in my area and the contractors pay me a commission on any work secured through my business. Best of all, the service is free to the homeowner.

Are there any requirements for this kind of business?

It helps to be organized and outgoing. I operate my business 90% by telephone however the majority of my time is spent talking with my contractors, my clients (homeowners) and networking for new leads in my community.

Any Start-up costs?

The operating costs are minimal. This is a word of mouth type of business and doesn't require a lot of money for advertising. Operating an HRN will require a phone, a computer and a fax.

I've documented my business model in a comprehensive manual, which I sell to other entrepreneurs looking for a viable home based business. The manual may be purchased individually or as a part of an HRN Business Package including one on one consultation time, forms promote items and a website. Packages range from $1795 to $3590.

What are your rates?

I've documented my business model in a comprehensive manual, which I sell to other entrepreneurs looking for a viable home based business. The manual may be purchased individually or as a part of an HRN Business Package including one on one consultation time, forms, promote items and a website. Packages range from $1795 to $3590.

What services do you provide?

An HRN is an organized referral service for homeowners comprised of highly skilled, pre-screened independent home improvement contractors. Contractors in the network may range from painters, plumbers and electricians to floor refinishers, carpenters a handymen. The value proposition that the HRN offers to the market is similar to that of a "broker". It is a reliable source for dependable service providers who are able to satisfy any homeowner need. The value proposition that an HRN offers to contractors is that of an "outsourced" sale and marketing force. The HRN takes on the responsibility of promoting their services to homeowners.

For those interested in launching a home based business, The Complete Guide To Owning And Operating A Successful Homeowner

Referral Network© is a comprehensive business manual, which documents every aspect of the HRN business. The manual outlines step-by-step procedures on how to launch a network in your area including detailed information on how to locate, screen and represent a comprehensive network of home improvement contractors, contractor commission structures, a comprehensive direct mail and advertising campaign, liability information, accounting procedures, insurance information and more.

The information provided in the HRN business manual allows others to duplicate my referral business in their area and launch a successful Homeowner Referral Network in a matter of weeks.

How do you market your business?

I market my services locally to homeowners in my area through a comprehensive direct mail campaign and networking in my community.

Will you ever expand?

It's my goal to make the Homeowner Referral Network (HRN) business a household name so that when homeowners nationally are interested in finding a reliable home improvement contractor, they know to look for an HRN operating in their area.

Do you have any tips for other mothers?

I recommend creating a mental (or written) checklist about you before deciding on any type of business. Ask yourself questions like, What are my abilities? What do I enjoy? How much am I willing to invest in a business both personally and financially? Do I have the discipline necessary to work from home?

By choosing a business, which maximizes your abilities and custom tailored to your needs, you'll increase your odds at success.

How do you balance your kids and your business?

I break my day into segments, which I devote, exclusively to work or exclusively to my family. I realized (the hard way) that you couldn't do everything at the same time. I wake up before my children and work for an hour or two. I work when they are in school, during nap times and when my husband is at home. There are times when its difficult to balance both but I always try to prioritize and my family comes first.

How about your spouse?

My husband is my biggest cheerleader as well as my biggest source of support and encouragement. We took a loan against his retirement savings plan so that I could launch Home Remedies and he brags that "I'm the best investment he's ever made!"

What is your biggest challenge?

The most important lesson that I've learned in launching my own business is that, regardless of how large or small you intend your business to be, you should build upon a solid foundation. Create a business plan, research competition, define who your customers are, investigate the various legal structures and seek the advice of reliable advisors who can guide you through the start up process.

I never expected my business to grow so quickly and fortunately I had established a Board of Advisors to help me deal with issues as they arose. Had it not been for their good advice I probably wouldn't have known to take certain measures to protect my business and myself.

Any rewards for doing this?

By far, the greatest reward is enjoying a stimulating career while staying at home to raise my children.

Any other advice for mothers?

There are no "get rich quick" schemes out there. Whatever you chose to do will require hard work and discipline but the keep in mind that the rewards of developing a successful business from "the ground up" are fantastic!

Debra's contact information:

Debra M. Cohen
Home Remedies of NY, Inc.™
Homeowner Referral Network (HRN) Business
"An Ideal Work From Home Solution"
Web: **http://www.homereferralbiz.com**
e-mail: homremdies@aol.com
Tel/Fax: 516-374-8504

COMPUTER SERVICE SPECIALIST

Name: Diana Ennen
Business: Ennen's Computer Services
Website: **http://www.gate.net/~gregnn**

In Diana's business, she specializes in word processing, virtual assisting and computer tutoring.

Why did Diana start her business?

I started my business 16 years ago when my son was born. I wanted to stay home with him and not work outside of the home and be away from him all day. Also, I felt with my prior secretarial skills that I had the skills necessary to be successful.

I absolutely love it. In addition to getting the chance to see my son grow and be a big part of his life, I think it's also had a very positive effect on him. He's seen me grow my business and knows what it's like to follow your dreams. I've since had two additional children.

Are there any requirements for this kind of business?

The main requirements are the ability to type well and also to proof your work well. If you choose to do virtual assisting, then you would want a good understanding of the Internet. For computer tutoring, you would want to know several software programs well.

Any Start-up costs?

It all depends on what you presently have. Since most people already have a computer, the main thing they will need is a good printer, transcriber, fax machine, business cards, money for advertising and licensing. I would say you could easily get started for approximately $1000.00 or less. Also, you don't absolutely need to have everything at the beginning. You can start out small and expand.

What are your rates?

Most word processors today charge $25.00 to $40.00 an hour.

What services do you provide?

I provide legal, medical and general transcription, typing of all correspondence, including resumes, academic papers, etc., computer tutoring on most of the major software programs, and also marketing of my books.

For my word processing business I do word processing for several attorneys, a chiropractor, a produce company, an international employment recruiter, resume clients, and many more. Those are just my main clients. However, in the past I've typed practically everything from school papers to manuscripts. If it needs to be typed, I'll type it. For the computer tutoring aspect of it, I do tutoring on most of the major software programs.

How do you market your business?

I initially sent out business letters to my targeted group and to all new businesses in the area that I felt could utilize my services. I stopped by printers and local businesses in the area and dropped off my business card and/or portfolio. I advertised in local weekly newspapers and in the Yellow Pages. I placed flyers up at colleges and advertised in their newspapers. I get up a web site and listed with all the major search engines. Also word of mouth was a big help. I contacted past employers, friends, business associates, etc., and let them know that I was starting a business and would appreciate their business.

Will you ever expand?

I have expanded over the years and added different aspects into my business including the virtual assisting and computer tutoring. I also have two back-up assistants to help when I get overwhelmed with work.

Do you have any tips for other mothers?

Believe in yourself and don't get discouraged. Start fresh every week with the determination that you will make this business a success. Learn as much as you can able the business and continue learning. The more you know, the more successful you can be. Learn to say no and keep control of your business. But, most importantly, have fun. Many start this business to spend more time with their children. Make sure that you don't get so busy that you forget that.

How do you balance your kids and your business?

That can be a challenge, especially in the summer months. But the main thing I do is to stay focused. When I'm at work I concentrate on work and when I'm with the family, I concentrate on them. By not being distracted I tend to do a better job. It also helps to be very organized. That way you don't waste valuable time looking for things.

Also, I try and make sure they have things available to keep them busy. New bead sets to make jewelry, craft kits, hook rug, etc. I also try and spend good quality time with them. We are very family oriented so we do a lot together. If I ever have a really busy week that requires more hours, I'll make it up to them by heading to the beach or taking them to a movie. Something special that shows them that I appreciate their letting me work. I also get them involved in the business whenever possible. For example if I'm sending out a mailer, my daughter can help stuff the envelopes. My son helps me by sending out book orders. The 4-year-old is still a little young, but what I'll do is get her a spare box of envelopes with labels and she can pretend to help.

How about your spouse?

He has always been extremely supportive of my business and proud of me as well. That really means a lot.

What is your biggest challenge?

Setting your limitations and not taking on too much work. Sometimes clients can get demanding and you need to be able to assert yourself. For example I once had a client whom would always request rush jobs, which caused me a lot of undo stress. Even though I charge extra for rush jobs, it was still hard to get the work done and keeps all my other clients happy. Once in a while it was okay, but it got to the point where it was constant. I finally had to tell him no on many occasions and I found that once I started saying no, he was able to get the work that needed to be typed to me in a reasonable time frame.

Any rewards for doing this?

There are so many rewards. I absolutely love what I do and can't imagine ever doing anything else. There's a tremendous satisfaction in owning a business. Most of my clients over the years have turned into good friends and often I feel I've been able to be a part of the success of their business. My hours are flexible so I can stay home with the kids if they are sick or just if we want to take the day off and go to the beach we can. Plus I truly believe it's instilled in them the belief that they can achieve their goals if they work hard for them. A lot of kids don't even realize what their parents do for a living, but mine have been an active part of my business and know most of my clients.

Any other advice for mothers?

I guess the biggest piece of advice would be to make sure that this is the right business for you. You will be so much more of a success if you do. Plus you will want to put forth the extra effort to make it successful.

Diana's contact information:

Diana is also the author of Words From Home; How to Start and Operate Your Own Home-Based Word Processing Business; Up Close and Virtual: The Practical Guide to Starting a Virtual Assisting Business and the Bizymoms Cookbook.

http://www.gate.net/~gregnn, DeeEnnen@aol.com,
(954) 782-0581.

CRAFTSMAKER

Name: Mary Miller
Business: Mary Miller Designs and Miller Pin Art
Website: **http://www.millerpinart.com** and **http://www. marymillerdesigns.com**

In Mary's business, she makes jewelry and other crafts, which she sells on and off-line.

Why did Mary start her business?

I was a working Mom with 2 grade school daughters and had worked in the insurance industry for 12 years. My husband and I had planned private education for our children and when we purchased our home the school district did not matter at that time. My oldest daughter wanted to attend public school when she entered the 3rd grade and all went well until my oldest daughter entered middle school. At that time my youngest daughter was in the 3rd grade. My oldest daughter had problems with the behavior of some of the males in the school who thought they could have their way with her and that went against her Christian belief. I found myself away from my office and in the counselor's office defending my daughter and our Christian beliefs more than I was in my office. I did not attend college after high school and three years prior to the middle school problems with my daughter; I had gone to our community college and graduated after age 40 with an accounting and computer degree. My husband and I discussed in length and detail my quitting work and home schooled my children in a Christian atmosphere. We entered our children in private school for one more year and then I left the workforce and we began home schooling. The girls and I really bonded and it was a lot of fun and dedication and lots of motivation on my part. At the present, my oldest has graduated high school and completed college with a Medical Office Administration degree. My youngest is a junior this year and all is going well. After we started our home schooling curriculum, we found it did not take the whole day to get the required subjects covered. We found a support group and joined them each week for our outing and fun time. We still had time on our hands and at this time I could use a little more cash in the household, as my salary was no longer there. I attended a Jewelry Show with my mother-in-law and found jewelry that I saw that I could make. I found a supply catalog lying on the floor behind one of the counters and the vendor told me to take it home with me thus started my home business of Miller Pin Art. I purchased parts and the girls and I started making Angel Pins (my husband wanted in on all the fun we were having so he created some Angels in the beginning and I still have a few of his large ones on hand which brings back memories. I found that I liked the small Angels but both sizes sold. The girls and I signed up for several crafts shows and traveled with our products and had "School on Wheels" from time to time during our travels as they had ample room in my van or the hotel room to do their school work. We opened booths in several craft malls in our surrounding area and supplied the booths as needed with our products. Two years ago, I decided to open a webstore on the web after a friend agreed to be my webmaster, as I knew nothing about being a webmaster. That has kept us busy, but recently an opportunity was landed in my lap, which I know that the Good Lord had a big hand in. I now have a way to be in touch with people and give and receive blessings from in the form of a storefront. I have just opened Miller's Hodge Podge a few miles from my home. I have antiques, glassware, jewelry and miscellaneous old and new stuff in my new shop that I open up half a week. This has been opened up to help when I suffer the empty cradle syndrome as my youngest daughter will graduate next year and I will have this to work my way through that. I feel fortunate that I have worked out of the home, then was able to work in the home when my children needed me and now that they are about to be on their own, I still have an outlet to get back in the workforce. I am truly a blessed person.

Are there any requirements for this kind of business?

I cannot stress self-motivation enough when you start a home business. Being the oldest of 7 children, I was made responsible at an early age and self-motivation has come easy for me. Responsibility for good record keeping can be a challenge if you have younger children in the home. Their demands of your time and energy will seem enormous at times, but with good quality self-motivation and responsibility will go a long way in the success of your home business. I find it easy to have several projects at one time going and get them all completed, but this does not come easy to some people.

Any Start-up costs?

Once you research and decide upon the home business that you wish to open, your first step would be to get a tax id number from your comptroller office. The next item to consider is where you plan to operate your home business in the home. If you can use an extra bedroom or your garage, you would then have the deduction for home office. You will need to have the funds available for your first order for your business project. There is always the Small Business Administration in your area that will offer you information on guidelines that you can follow and after completing them, they will help you secure financing with the banking establishments that they work with. I have found the Small Business Administration to be very helpful and supportive to me in all my business endeavors.

What are your rates?

There is lots of researching to get the best rates for any project or business that you plan on opening. With the Stock Market the way it is now, it is very dependent upon the individual as to the rate you will have to pay.

What services do you provide?

I provide a 100% customer satisfaction guarantee on all my products as they are handmade. I provide PayPal account and Visa and Mastercard accounts through a merchant account that you will need to set up. There are merchant accounts on the net that you can subscribe to instead of setting up your own account. If I want to increase sales, I can set my site up for free shipping from time to time. I also offer mail in orders from my site for the ones that are not comfortable using their card numbers on the net.

How do you market your business?

I used search engines and ezines that offered free ads when I first started. I used this for the first six months or so. I would set aside a few hours a week and send out ads for my website. I eventually used a few of the paid ads from a few sites that complemented my site and by that time I was receiving offers for free and paid ads. I went to my local sign vendor and purchased the removable magnetic signs to stick on my van doors advertising my website which also had my phone number and led to many phone orders and web orders.

Will you ever expand?

I did expand in about six months after opening the Miller Pin Art website and opened a sister site Mary Miller Designs and offered a free jewelry contest which brought in lots of email with addresses, etc. for my future use. My plans in the future is to start an ezine from my website and then do desktop publishing for publishing a monthly booklet with paid advertising for my local entrepreneurs.

Do you have any tips for other mothers?

I have no tips for other mothers with young children, as I have not been in their shoes, but any mothers who have grade school children or teens, I will be happy to talk with them and answer any questions that they may have. I have been there, done that, and have succeeded with my sanity intact. As I stated previously, self-motivation and responsibility to get the job done is the major most important quality that you need to have to succeed.

How do you balance your kids and your business?

Times can get very stressful at times and you will have times of thinking that there is no balance of kids and business. Your website business can be worked prior to their waking or after the children have retired. Scheduling is very important to keep a balance between the two. I found that quality time set aside from home schooling and webstore and booth activities was very important to my children. Guidelines will have to be set up and timelines will have to be followed to keep an even flow going between your family and home business. When the girls wanted to go shopping and I had a pressing business matter to take care of, they have stated a few times that they were not as important as my business. In their heart, they knew better, but being together 24/7, the stress level could start to rise from time to time.

How about your spouse?

I have a very supportive spouse who has supported me in any home business, net or store front that I have desired to operate. Of course, you have to make time for your spouse although your mind may be on another business matter or project that you are presently working on. You can share things that the children have done with him and let him in on your thoughts for your business. You can bond together on these family entities that interest you both.

What is your biggest challenge?

The biggest challenge would be to set your mind that "yes you can have a home business" if you really desire this. You can have both a family and a home business if you have the self-motivation that it takes. If you set your mind that this can be done, then get out there and do it and reap the rewards.

Any rewards for doing this?

Besides the financial rewards, you will have the reward of being with your family when they need you. Down the road, after you are established, you will have the reward of satisfaction that you have completed and succeeded in your home business. You will also have the reward of all the many friends you will meet as you come into contact with so many nice people in getting your home business set up and running.

Any other advice for mothers?

Again, I stress that with self-motivation, you can succeed in a home business. You will have to work your home business as a professional business and not let your home surroundings side tract you, which will happen often. Set your mind that this is what you want and your family needs and by all means, go for it.

Mary's contact information:

http://www.millerpinart.com
http://www.marymillerdesigns.com and meet my products and me.
You will find my contact information at the end of each website, but I will include it here also:
Mary Miller,
P.O. Box 1533,
Groves, Texas 77619
(409) 962-7155
If in Texas, visit me for some fun shopping pleasures at:
Miller's Hodge Podge,
1302 Pt. Neches Ave.,
Pt. Neches, Texas 77651
1 (409) 724-6166

Baby Blankets

Name: Lisa Barnes
Business: Baby Bee Inc.
Website: **http://www.babybeeinc.com**

In Lisa Barnes business, she designs soft and comfy baby blankets.

Why did Lisa start her business?

It all started when I received a gift of handmade flannel baby blankets from a friend of mine. They were so soft and beautiful, and the fact that she'd made them herself made them a very special gift. I just fell in love with these blankets and I could hardly wait for Macy to be born so I could wrap her in them.

I began making similar blankets for friends and family as gifts. The response to them was overwhelming and I soon had several people asking me to make more so they could give them as gifts. Quite often when I was sewing these blankets, I would daydream about making a business of it. I could see the perfect blanket in my mind and I knew there was nothing else out there exactly like the custom blankets I wanted to create and I knew that once the word was out, they'd be a big hit. I wanted it to be a business that I could run from home so I could continue to be home with Macy. I wanted to, if possible, to have the sewing done by stay-at-home moms so they could continue to stay home with their children. I wanted to find a way to not only sell these blankets as the perfect baby gift that they are, but I also wanted it to be a business that would benefit children in some way.

Finally I decided it was time to give it a try. I spent any spare moments I had, preparing, researching, planning and compiling the information I needed to start this business. I sat down at the kitchen table and sketched out the happy little "Baby Bee" you see on our sew-in labels and hang tags. I also designed a few prototypes of my version of "the perfect baby blanket." I wanted them to be unique in everything from dimensions to fabric combinations, to colors and packaging. What I came up with was a "kid-sized," 40"x 40" blanket with beautifully coordinated fabrics, made from the softest 100% cotton flannel, reversible, and quilt-stitched for durability and washable. Each one would have one of our cheerful Baby Bee labels sewn into the corner of the blanket, and a custom hang tag hanging from our trademark coordinating "scrunchie" that secures each blanket. My plan was to have as many styles to choose from as possible. I started with 8 styles and as of today, I'm up to 20 styles and growing!

In November of 1999, the Baby Bee, Inc. website was launched.

Are there any requirements for this kind of business?

As with any business, I think the basic requirements are just to do your homework. To take the time to research every aspect you can think of that would apply to your business. For me it was things like fabric pricing, sewing costs, shipping, website design and maintenance, advertising, etc. Also check in to the market you want to reach. Is there a demand for your product? What about your competition—what do they have to offer? Does your product stand out from the crowd? Once you have a good idea of these types of things, you can more realistically assess the feasibility of your particular business.

Any Start-up costs?

I wish I could say that I started it on a shoestring, but there were so many things I needed to get this business going. My goal was to start it for under $10,000 and I was able to get Baby Bee, Inc. up and running for just over $8,500.00. I am fortunate to have a wonderful husband who believed in my big ideas and agreed to use some of our savings to start the business.

What are your rates?

Our main blanket line, the 40"x40" custom flannel, is the type of blanket you'd find in an upscale baby boutique for $40.00 and up. With our blankets priced at only $32.95 each, I feel great about the value that we are able to offer our customers. We offer giftwrap services at $2.95 for one blanket and $3.95 for three or more blankets. Shipping is $6.00 for one blanket and $2.00 for each additional blanket going to the same address.

What services do you provide?

We provide a very quick and easy way to shop for a really great baby blanket. For added convenience, we also offer a custom giftwrap ensemble and personalized gift card. In most cases we ship our orders the same day if received by 2:00 p.m. or at least within 24 hours. The comments we've received from our customers have been extremely positive regarding our products, the ease of shopping at the Baby Bee, Inc. website and the quick turn around time.

How do you market your business?

At present, Baby Bee, Inc. is marketed by submission to the search engines, links to related websites and by word of mouth. It's done pretty well with just this, but I am always looking into other avenues of marketing such as opt-in e-mail lists, e-zines, automated search engine positioning software and possibly some print ads in related magazines.

Will you ever expand?

Yes! I do add fun new styles to the custom flannel line on a regular basis and at any given time, we usually have 20+ different styles to choose from. I'd like to get it to at least 30+ styles and I'd like to further expand by someday adding blankets made of different types of fabrics. Possibly gift sets and related items also. As always, a major focus will be placed on finding ways to get our fleece blankets donated to needy children in the U.S. and abroad. There are countless children out there who are suffering from things like abuse, poverty, neglect, abandonment, homelessness, major illness, etc. I want to let these little ones know that someone cares about them. I want to offer them hope, comfort and love in the form of a cozy security blanket.

Do you have any tips for other mothers?

If I could give advice to someone wanting to start an Internet business, it would be not to fall for the popular misconception that if you have a great product, that you can just design a website, submit it to the search engines and the orders will start rolling in. In 99.9% of cases, there is no "instant success" on the Internet. There's a considerable amount of hard work involved, but it can be very rewarding if you stick with it. You need to find a niche—create or find a product that is unique, that there is a demand for. Study your competition and find a way to stand out from them in everything from products offered to customer service to website design. Be committed to your product and be ready to persevere.

How do you balance your kids and your business?

I am happy to say that today I am having lots of fun running a steadily growing business which I am able to run from home without cutting into my "mom and wife" time. Macy likes to help out with everything from packing orders to holding the door open at the post office when my arms are overloaded with blankets to be mailed.

Being the mother of a small child and a wife does make running this business a little challenging at times, but we always make it work. I try to do most of my work when my daughter is at preschool, also, I tend to be a night owl, so working at night is a natural fit for me. My husband is out of town for business one or more days per week, so I take advantage of that time to work also. As I mentioned in part one, Macy does like to help out sometimes, with processing orders and donations. She enjoys doing things like handing me blankets to be wrapped, counting out hang tags, helping to tape packages and put on mailing labels, etc.

Of course there are times when she, like most 5-year-olds, would rather be playing with her friends. Because she is an only child and because we live in an area where there are no children her age to play with, I will once in awhile take her to the home of a good friend of mine, Macy absolutely loves to go there. This works out great because it gives Macy time to play and be with other children and it gives me a little more time to work on the company. There is only one problem with this though and it is that she has so much fun there that it is hard to get her to leave! Anyway, there seems to be a nice balance between this business and family life at this point and Baby Bee, Inc. is running at a very manageable, family-friendly pace.

How about your spouse?

I have experienced setbacks and discouragement at times, but I have my wonderful husband to thank for his unwavering support, and for always encouraging me to refocus and to go forward.

What is your biggest challenge?

With all the responsibilities and distractions of family life, I have found that my biggest challenge is just staying focused. It's sometimes hard to find uninterrupted blocks of time to sit and think things through, and to do all that needs to be done to keep this business on course. Staying motivated is another challenge. Let's face it, starting and running your business is not always a walk in the park. It's a learning experience that can sometimes be very frustrating. But on the other hand, a rave review from a customer, a new word-of-mouth referral, or the realization that thousands of children have been wrapped in, snuggled with, and comforted by our blankets tends to put me quickly back on track.

Any rewards for doing this?

I am happy to say that today I am having lots of fun running a steadily growing business which I am able to run from home without cutting into my "mom and wife" time.

Any other advice for mothers?

My advice would be to save yourself lots of time, money and headaches by just taking the time to do the research and by not being afraid to ask lots of questions of potential web design companies.

Lisa's contact information:

BABY BEE, INC.
BABY BLANKETS EXTRAORDINAIRE!
1 (800) 927-3834

Childcare Provider

Name: Cindy Clark
Business: Building Blocks Family Daycare
Website: **www.geocities.com/heartland/prairie/2091**

In Cindy's business, she owns and runs a family childcare business.

Why did Cindy start her business?

I had worked outside the home since graduating from high school, working my way up through the ranks of work-study student to secretary to administrative assistant. I thought I would be a "lifer" because the pay was good, the benefits were great and I couldn't imagine doing anything else. But after 16 years of working and two children later, I got pregnant with my third child and everything changed. My mother-in-law had a daycare and that's where my two boys went. But this time around I decided I would like to be home because I finally figured out I was missing some of my kids' childhood. So I took an informational class offered by the Center for Childcare Resources and I was hooked! I decided owning my own business was just the thing for me.

Are there any requirements for this kind of business?

Although in my state there are no specific qualifications or requirements, I chose to become state-registered, become a member of the Child and Adult Care Food Program, and take a series of ChildNet classes to understand the various aspects of running a home daycare. The ages and stages of children and present a professional image, among other topics. It also helps if you like to be around children all day, have experience in communication and business practices. The main thing I'd suggest you have when running your own daycare is patience. If you don't currently have any of these skills, don't despair—, as there are classes, associations, and mentors to help strengthening any weaknesses every step of the way.

Any Start-up costs?

Start-up costs are minimal, especially if you have your own children. You may want to purchase toys, a high chair, pack 'n play or crib, or other age-appropriate items if you don't already have them. But keep track of any purchases you make so you can record them for your taxes.

What are your rates?

Rates can vary from area to area. Generally, rates fall between $70-120 per child per week. You can charge more if you offer specific care such as infants only, after-school only, night services, etc.

What services do you provide?

Loving and nurturing care. Age appropriate activities, large and small motor skills, music activities, etc. Plus communicating with the parents every day so they know what their child learned or what we did in day-care.

How do you market your business?

There are several things you can do to market your business. In fact, Redleaf National Institute has written a book on how to market your daycare. See **www.redleafinstitute.com**. Besides the general word-of-mouth and newspaper advertising, you can print up T-shirts, mugs, bookmarks, pencils, etc. and hand these out at garage sales, Halloween, doctor's offices, and the list is endless. I would recommend purchasing this book for GREAT information. So being home, you have time to develop other interests or pursue your hobbies!

Will you ever expand?

The great thing about daycare is that your business can be as small or large as you are comfortable with, within the accepted regulations in your area. This means taking in one child or possibly up to five, plus after-school children.

Do you have any tips for other mothers?

If you really want to be home with your children and still need to bring in an income, daycare can be a great option. You don't need any special skills other than a love for children, but there are many opportunities to gain knowledge and grow in your field. I have taken my daycare business one step beyond and now teach ChildNet classes. I also write articles based on my experience in daycare, which are published in national newsletters. I've found that even "doing daycare" can lead to so many neat things. I had my picture in the July issue of Ladies' Home Journal in an article about what women earn. I have written a cookbook "Freezer Cooking for Daycare Providers" which is available at **www.30daygourmet.com**. Also, you will find you have extra time to do laundry, make meals, and other things you normally have to accomplish on weekends or evenings when you work outside the home. If one of your goals is to have more family time, doing daycare can really help.

How do you balance your kids and your business?

I have found that my children adapt well to having other playmates around during the day. Even if they aren't the same age, everyone learns by being around children of all ages. My kids have their rooms as their personal space, no daycare children are allowed in there if they need some quiet time. I have personal days written into the daycare contract that allow me to attend my kids' field trips or school events that occur during the day. This way I don't miss out on their events or make them feel that business is more important than they are.

How about your spouse?

My spouse is very supportive of the daycare. He fully understands this is my business and I run ideas off him. He has helped in every way imaginable and has realized the benefits if me being home.

What is your biggest challenge?

The biggest challenge in doing daycare is getting the parents to treat you like a business. They sometimes have the "baby-sitter" mentality and think you are their employee and they can set the rules. It's just the opposite. You are the business owner, you set the rules, and the parents need to respect that. They can, and sometimes do, try to get you to compromise on every little issue. This is where you need to have a strong contract and review it thoroughly with them before you agree to care for their child.

Any rewards for doing this?

There are many rewards of having your own childcare. You get to be home with your children, you have the opportunity to teach and nurture other children, and you meet many people. You can make a decent living, have the benefit of setting all the rules, pay scale, schedule, etc.

Any other advice for mothers?

I would suggest that before jumping into childcare, you do a little research. Find out going rates in your area. Get your spouse's support. Take a few informational classes. Write down the pros and cons of doing childcare compared to what you are currently doing. Join a daycare association or check with your local Extension Office to see what other support is available. If you decide this is the career for you, then do everything in your power to make it the best business you can. You will be far happier if you do.

Cindy's contact information:

I have a website with articles for anyone interested in doing daycare at

www.geocities.com/heartland/prairie/2091

Feel free to e-mail me and ask questions about starting your business.

Business Organizer

Name: Michelle Johnson
Business: Work From The Hearth
Website: **http://www.workfromthehearth.com**

In Michelle's business, she created a computerized contact organizer, ad tracking, and co-op management system.

Why did Michelle start her business?

Upon the birth of my first daughter, my world was turned inside out. Instead of being the die-hard career woman I had envisioned, I was turned instantly into a dress-wearing, craft-making, cookie-baking homemaker…and I LOVED it! I wanted nothing more than to stay home and savor every moment of my daughter's life and be the world's most perfect mom to the world's most perfect little girl (I now have a second little perfection…).

I am a stay at home mom first, but still thought it would be nice to add to our family income IF I could find a business that would work around my life. I looked for a legitimate work at home business for over three years, ran into some amazing scams, and finally found The MOM Team, which is paired with a wonderful manufacturer of household products, in November of 2001. Determined to succeed, I launched myself into it full force (that is, over naptime). I placed dozens of Internet ads, flyers, created postcards, and participated in a high-end co-op. I immediately signed up six new people and was considered a great success and real up-and-comer. The co-op brought me in 80 leads in a matter of weeks and from the outside, my business was soaring.

On the inside, however, my business was floundering in a disorganized mess. The business I started is an amazing opportunity with incredible support, which completely lacks any of the fundamental tools necessary for success. I don't know of a single successful corporation that keeps track of clients and prospects on paper.

So, there I was I had contacts, but no contact manager. My leads were falling through the cracks. I had ads, but no effective system for tracking them. I lost track of which ones expired and if I had paid for them. As the leads poured in from the co-op, my excitement grew into dread. I couldn't remember what I had said or when to follow up with them.

That's when I stopped everything and my husband and I created a computerized contact organizer, ad tracking, and co-op management system for me and the people in my organization. It wasn't long before we realized that, with a lot of hard work, we could put our system on the Internet for people with other work at home businesses to use. Seven months later Work From The Hearth was successfully launched.

Are there any requirements for this kind of business?

To start any business, you simply need to be able to identify a true need in a market that you are familiar with. It is best when the business utilizes skills you currently have, or have available. If you must learn new skills, make sure they aren't daunting, or that you are willing to rise to the challenge if they are.

Any Start-up costs?

Our domain cost $14 to start and $10 per month thereafter. We also spent several hundred dollars on advertising. Websites are very inexpensive to start and maintain, as long as you have the programming knowledge to create them.

What are your rates?

Our service is $4.95/mo for basic and $9.95/mo for preferred. We will remain inexpensive so we can be affordable to the newest work at home entrepreneur. Our charge simply covers advertising, growth, and maintenance of the site.

What services do you provide?

Contact organization, Ad tracking, and co-op management. We are working on a scheduling tool right now.

How do you market your business?

We offer partnerships to other sites that compliment our tools and exchange links and banners with them. We place paid ads every chance we get. I have experienced no success with free ads.

Will you ever expand?

Yes! We are incorporating a detailed scheduling section right now, and would like to add an inventory and distribution section for businesses that sell products. We have many more plans for our business, but I'm not at liberty to discuss them at this juncture.

Do you have any tips for other mothers?

Keep your priorities straight. Write them down and post them on the wall. If your first priority is your family, and your child interrupts your business for some family time…look up and read what your priorities are. Live every minute inside of those priorities and everything else will fall into place.

How do you balance your kids and your business?

Our first priority is our family, period. We wanted to start this business but didn't want it to usurp our family time. My husband woke at 5am every day to work a couple of hours before he left for his full-time job. I worked over our girls' nap times. We would both work again once the girls were in bed for the night. We decided we wanted to do this business…our children didn't. We understood that we would rather have success come slower and capture every day with our children than miss any one of them.

How about your spouse?

He not only supports me, but also is the creator of our website. We altered our "together time" to include working on our business. It's a project we can do together and has been wonderful!

What is your biggest challenge?

The biggest challenges have absolutely been TIME and money! This is something we could have had completed in only a couple of months had we put our family on hold. Instead, though, we made sure our family didn't sacrifice and it took over 8 months to create our site and we are working on new features still. My husband just graduated with his MBA in December (two months after the start of Work From The Hearth) and we have been recovering from that financial strain. That has limited our marketing budget pretty significantly and we've had to work around those constraints.

Any rewards for doing this?

I have loved using our site! It's been wonderful to have loads of information at my fingertips. Our biggest reward, though, would definitely have to be in watching other home business owners get organized. Every extra minute they spend with their family because of their new organization is pure success to us.

Any other advice for mothers?

I just can't stress enough to write down your priorities, post them on your wall, and judge your daily actions based on those priorities. Live within your priorities and you will be happy. Being happy, you have already achieved success.

Michelle's contact information:

Work From The Hearth (**www.workfromthehearth.com**) is the only affordable online organizing tool for home business owners. Every inch of our site is customizable to fit your home business needs, free of charge. Allow your business to maintain itself while you concentrate on growing it.

Michelle@workfromthehearth.com

NETWORK DIRECTOR

Name: Sharon S. E. Schlossenberg
Business: My Woman2Woman Network
Website: **http://www.mywoman2woman.com**

Sharon's business involves promoting women in small businesses.

Why Sharon started her business.

I began working at home for a virtual concierge company several years ago. This past year my job description changed and I was no longer able to fulfill my duties from home. I tried to return to the outside work force, however my 4 year old son has ADHD and was unable to remain in childcare, and quite frankly I didn't want him or my other children there anyway. I started to look for another work at home position and then decided that it was time for me to start my own business. I began Kidz Koncierge and formed many relationships with other women in the same stages. I started a "Products Partner" page and from there grew My Woman2Woman Network.

Are there any requirements for this kind of business?

The real qualification for running a network is being able to interact with people on a personal level. If you don't get along well with people, can't relate or empathize you won't do well in this field.

Any Start-up costs?

The costs are web hosting, site design if you don't know how, (I suggest buying FrontPage and learning how to do it yourself. You'll save a bundle in the end!). Additional costs can be ad-free message boards, advertising, printing cost if you have a print newsletter, postage, and so on depending on what features you offer. If you don't have a computer yet, you'll definitely need one of those! Your computer needs depend on your business, but whatever you do you'll need a printer. I suggest a

3-in-1, printer, scanner and fax, it will also save you money in the long run.

What are your rates?

I earn revenue through several methods, first membership dues. At this time we have two levels, Silver and Gold. The fees are currently $45 and $65 but are going up this fall. I also sell advertising space on our site, and our newsletter.

What services do you offer?

I provide members with unique marketing opportunities, such as our e-catalogue. Instead of a traditional paper catalogue we create a page for members and burn it on a CD to be distributed, this allows a view to click directly on the members link and go right to their site instead of having to remember the URL and visiting it later. Instant gratification! Each of our members has their own webpage on our site as well.

How do you market your business?

Honestly, our best marketing tool is our members. Word of mouth and member referrals have been wonderful for My W2W.

Will you ever expand?

YES! We are currently expanding. We have several new sites, My Woman Expo is going to be hosting live, local Expos all over the US and hopefully Canada by next year. Our first Expo is this October in Rosemont, IL. Not only will there be vendors at the Expos, but also free workshops to teach women how to start and market their own business. In additional we are starting My Girlfriend2Girlfriend, a fun sun for women (no kid talk allowed!), Just4Girlfriends, an intimate site for women (over 18 only), Lets Swap, a site for bartering, wholesaling and franchise opportunities. Aside from the W2W Network I will be expanding my personal business, Kidz Koncierge, to include a toy store and party place. We have also recently added a travel partner.

Do you have any tips for other mothers?

Don't wait to start your own business. You will always find excuses to put it off, trust me; there is no time like the present! It is hard and frustrating and the kids will get into things while you are in the middle of something, but it is worth it. Something to remember when the kids are driving you crazy is that they are one of the main reasons you want to be home, so don't be too hard on them when they accidentally hang up the phone in the middle of an important business call.

How do you balance your kids and your business?

I try to cuddle with all of the kids in my bed every morning before we start the day, (That way I know they still feel loved when I'm yelling at them that afternoon, lol). I try to find things for them to do, but it doesn't usually work out. I've really had to become a clock-watcher to make sure that they get lunch on time or the day just flies by.

How about your spouse?

My spouse is pretty supportive. He is a man though so some times he's a little jealous of the computer. I get more work done when he's not home, you would think I would get more done when he's here to watch the kids, but not the case! I feel guilty for working when he's home, and if he takes the kids out to play so I can work it's too quiet for me to concentrate. I usually try and rap up everything before he gets home.

What is your biggest challenge?

The biggest challenge is usually my kids. However, recently my biggest challenges have been technical. My computer crashed and left me off line for several days, I'm actually using my daughter's computer right now because they sent mine back from the shop and they seem to have forgotten to fix the problem. If you are going to work online you really do need a back-up computer. Another must is Broadband or DSL. Dial up really is too slow for working online, in my opinion anyway.

Any rewards for doing this?

The number one reward, I'm home with my family. Second, I don't have to get dressed unless I want to. And the perks go on and on, I can put my feet on my desk, eat at my desk, sleep at my desk, I can even work from bed!

Any other advice for mothers?

Find something that you are passionate about, if you aren't excited about what you do, how can you expect anyone else to be? Try and create a schedule that is flexible, you're not wonder woman. Most of all remember to have fun and to enjoy yourself!

Sharon's contact information:

Sharon S. E. Schlossenberg
Director—My Woman2Woman Network
http://www.mywoman2woman.com
Email: **director@mywoman2woman.com**

PERSONALIZED BABY BLANKET DESIGNER

Name: Heidi Bowen
Business: BlankeeByHeidi
Website: **Http://BlankeebyHeidi.IsCute.com**

In Heidi's business, she designs personalized baby blankets. These are not your normal personalized baby blankets-they are exclusive! Each one is designed around the individual baby and his/her family. Each Blankee contains all the important birth information on the baby and the family and soon becomes a cherished piece of art that the entire family holds dear. She also publishes a parenting newsletter called The Blankee Bulletin.

Why did Heidi start her business?

I started my company for many reasons, as we all do. First of all, there is not a product like mine on the market. Secondly, I wanted to give my very best friend something more than a product I could buy off of any shelf in any store. Third, of course, I needed the money but still wanted to stay home with my children.

It all started when my very best friend became pregnant. I wanted to give her something no other new mom had but I didn't know what! She kept telling me that all she wanted was a blanket with a satin border. Well, being the type of person I am, I couldn't see myself only getting her a small blanket with a satin border, I HAD to get her something more! At the time, my 3rd baby had spent much time in the hospital from complications after his birth and he was still very sick. Needless to say, money was tight. When I went to the store to shop for my friend, I couldn't find anything that was completely and totally for her and the baby. Everything was so commercialized. I ended up getting her the blanket with the satin border that she wanted, but I was completely heart-broken when I couldn't find anything else that said what I wanted to say that was still with-in my price range. I drove to her baby shower with a heavy heart, feeling utterly horrible because she was my best friend and a simple little blanket was all I was giving to her on such an important day. The feeling worsened when I arrived at her shower and saw all the beautifully wrapped presents sitting on the display table. It wasn't until that very moment that I knew what I was going to do! I remembered that I had two small bottles of non-toxic fabric paint in my car. I asked my friend if I could use her bedroom so that I could work away from all of the children. She agreed and in about 45 minutes, I had created a beautiful pattern on the Blanket of little pink hearts with a mint green border. The pattern I created allowed room for all the members of the shower to sign a message to the baby. My friend absolutely loved her blanket and the very first Blankee by Heidi was born! Still to this day, over 10 years ago, that little girl begs her mother to pull out her Blankee by Heidi so she can read all the signatures and notes from all the people who were happily awaiting her arrival!

Since then, I have worked out of my home as a teacher for many years and although I loved my job, I truly feel it is more important for me to be at home with my children. Friends and family had coaxed me to start selling my Blankees for years and as you can see, they finally won. Two years ago, I opened my very own home-based business and named it: Blankee by Heidi! We now specialize in not only blankets, but also many different personalized gifts. We believe that gift giving is about the person you are giving the gift to. We design gifts that match your loved-one's personality, and the look on your loved-one's face when they receive your gift from Blankee by Heidi, makes it all worth it!

In our attempt to continue to help other mothers out there who are struggling with parental issues as well as starting their own home-based businesses, I also publish a newsletter called The Blankee Bulletin. One of the things that I have found to be the most difficult in my home-based business venture is finding advertising that actually works! Advertising that is geared to MY targeted audience and ads that don't get lost in a publication that is so huge, that I cannot even find my own ad when I am looking for it! The Blankee Bulletin is a small local publication full of tangible information all parents can use and products that our readers are interested in! I know how difficult it is to get your name out there and to get your business moving, and that is why I pride myself in taking things a step further for my advertisers. Not only do I make sure that every issue goes into the hand of a potential customer, but I also talk to those potential customers about my advertisers and their products. I believe that word-of-mouth advertising is one of the best forms of advertising available to us and if people hear your business name being recommended to someone, they are much more willing to look you up when they need you! As women and small business owners, we are all in this together. If we want people to take our businesses and our products seriously, we have to take ourselves seriously first.

Are there any requirements?

Creativity is about the only qualification I can think of. Since you do not have the cash flow of a major corporation, you have to come up with more creative ways to get the word out about your business!

Any Start-up costs?

For me, start-up costs were very little. I simply started with one Blankee by Heidi and once it sold, I created a few more. It was very slow at first but as it grew, I became faster at creating them so it worked out. Now that we are branching out into many other gifts, costs have escalated of course, but so far, we are able to keep up.

What services do you offer?

We design personalized, hand-drawn, hand-painted, customized Blankee by Heidi baby blankets and gifts. We also publish an awesome parenting newsletter called the Blankee Bulletin that provides work at home moms an excellent a cost effective advertising avenue.

How do you market your business?

I belong to numerous networking groups, advertise in local parenting publications, attend trade shows, and write articles for numerous parenting websites.

Will you ever expand?

Probably, at some point, but right now I am back in school working towards a degree in developmental neuro-psychology and I am not sure I could handle the business if it became any bigger.

Do you have any tips for other mothers?

Find your passion! Whatever that is, it makes the perfect home-based business! Not only that, but if you love what you do, you can get others to love it too and that helps you to create a client base that believes in you and your products! Involve your family in the planning process. Let them know you are serious and that you need their support.

How do you balance your kids and your business?

Wow! How do any of us balance life and a family? It isn't easy...I would have to say that we are a VERY scheduled family. Make time to work and make time to spend with your family. Plan vacations way out so that you all have something to look forward to. Eat dinner together every night, it offers you a wonderful opportunity to catch up!

How about your spouse?

My partner is probably the very best thing that ever happened to me! He is extremely supportive and acts as my one-man fan club when things get tough! I don't want you to feel that you must be with some-one to start a home-based business though. Many women start their businesses by themselves with the support of friends and family!

What is your biggest challenge?

Advertising! Getting my name out there in front of the people who want to buy my Blankees without breaking my budget!

Any rewards for doing this?

Being available when my kids need me. Anytime someone is sick or has an event going on at school there isn't any question, I am there!

Any other advice for mothers?

Read everything you possibly can on starting a home-based business. Check out online sources. Research your business fully so that you are prepared when you finally take the plunge. Be prepared to make yourself stop working and spend time with your family. After all, they are the whole reason you decided to do this in the first place!

Heidi's contact information:

My website is located at: **Http://BlankeebyHeidi.IsCute.com**
Please feel free to contact me if you have any questions.
I don't have all the answers but I can usually point you in the right direction!

DIRECT SALES

Name: Kim Troutman
Business: The MOM Team
Website: **troutman@pacifier.com**

In Kim's business, she sells natural made products through direct sales.

Why did Kim start her business?

My name is Kim Troutman and I work with a great team of moms known as the MOM Team. We work with a company that manufactures safer alternatives to household products that we use each day. I have 3 little boys and a baby on the way next year. My kids are my main reason for getting started with this business, but I also wanted to supplement my husband's income. It made no sense to us, for me to have to go out and get a job, only to have my paycheck go to pay for daycare. I decided to look for something I could do from home, but all I found were scams. I found the MOM Team and thought it sounded good, and I really had nothing to lose. So I joined, and it was the best decision I think I ever made.

Are there any requirements for this kind of business?

Just determination and a willingness to learn! You don't have to be a mom either...we have several dads on our team as well. This isn't a get rich quick scheme, so as long as you are willing to learn and determined to succeed, you definitely qualify. The only thing required is a minimum monthly purchase of approx. $50USD in products that they have. These are things like personal hygiene items, laundry/cleaning supplies, makeup and vitamins. They are products you use everyday!

Any Start-up costs?

The start up cost is $29USD, and that gets you a 1 year membership into the company we work with and a business kit filled with tons of information about the company, income potential, ect. This fee is 100% guaranteed and fully refundable for up to 4 months. It's risk free and you have nothing to lose.

We help moms who want to stay home and raise their kids while earning an income at home. We give them a FREE website, FREE training, and support them at ALL times.

How do you market your business?

I market mainly online, but I have also made up flyers and I have business cards that I give out all the time. I try to stay away from FFA (free for all) sites, and classifieds. Most of those places are filled with scams or get rich quick schemes and I don't want anyone thinking that my opportunity is just another scam. I try to get on message boards, ezines, groups and newsletters. There are a lot of places to get the word out to moms, so that is where I try to market the MOM Team!

Will you ever expand?

My team is always growing. More and more people want to use safer products and improve their health, so I know my team will just take off one of these days! Right now I am a Marketing Executive, and I hope to be a Director III by the end of the year.

Do you have any tips for other Mothers?

If you are looking for a legitimate opportunity, I suggest you check everything out thoroughly before investing any money into it. Check the BBB as well, and if it sounds to good to be true... it probably is. I am a mom, and I have been a victim of scams. I got involved with the MOM Team, because their motto is Moms Helping Moms. I have lived up to that, I want to help moms reach their goals and accomplish dreams.

How do you balance your kids and your business?

My kids are young, so it can be a challenge some days. But I have a schedule that I try to stick to. I try to only work when my kids are taking a nap or when they go to bed at night. On the occasions that I have to work when they are awake, I tend to do ONLY the things that need my immediate attention, and put other things aside for a later time. If you have a schedule, it makes life a LOT easier. You learn to divide your time. But I know that working at home is the best thing I can do for my kids. I can play with them whenever I want to, and I can be there to kiss the boo-boos too. I love my job and my kids!

How about your spouse?

Another good thing about working at home, I can set my own hours. Since my husband works during the week and gets weekends off, that is my schedule as well. We have alone time and family time every weekend. My husband is very supportive of me, and has been even more so since he was able to scale his hours back a bit, because I'm bringing in some money now. Our relationship was very strong before and it still is even with the business.

What is your biggest challenge?

My biggest challenge is finding time to stop working. That may sound funny, but it's true. Once I start something, I find a hard time stopping. But, I know I have other things around the house that need to be done, so just like with the kids, I try to only do things that need immediate attention, and save the rest for after the housework is done, and the kids are in bed. Another reason why it's good to have a schedule!

Any rewards for doing this?

The best rewards are seeing my kids' everyday! Don't get me wrong, I enjoy getting a paycheck every month, but that isn't my biggest reward. My family means a lot to me, and that is why I got started in the first place. Yes I wanted to make money, but I wanted to be home for my kids-and I am!

Any other advice for mothers?

Just be careful what you get into. I can't stress that enough. I have been scammed so many times, and I hate to see it happen to other people...especially moms. The MOM Team is such a great group, and most of us have been though several scams, so we know what to look for. I'm not saying the MOM Team is the only legitimate business out there, just be careful and check things out.

Kim's contact information:

If you would like more information you can fill out the secure form on my website **http://kimtroutman.themomteam.com**

I'd be happy to contact you and answer any questions you may have. We are all just customers of a pharmaceutical company that makes safer products. We also save 30% on these products for being a preferred customer. You can choose to be a customer first, or start right out building a business. It's risk free! With the money back guarantee, you have nothing to lose!

Kim Troutman
(503) 842-7167
troutman@pacifier.com

Pre/postnatal Fitness Instructor

Name: Lisa Stone
Business: Fit For 2
Website: **http://www.fitfor2.com**

In Lisa's business, she is the owner of Fit For 2, which teaches pre/postnatal fitness classes.

Why did Lisa start her business?

When I moved from Los Angeles to Atlanta almost ten years ago, I was shocked to find no pre/postnatal fitness classes at any of the area health clubs or community centers. When I approached those facilities about offering classes, they were not interested and felt there was no need for them. I felt differently! Atlanta, after all, was Baby Central, and I saw so many people outside either walking or running that I knew a fitness class specifically designed for pregnant women and new moms would be successful. So, I found a community center with an aerobics room that was willing to let me rent the space a couple of hours a week, and I went into business.

Are there any requirements for this kind of business?

In order to teach Fit For 2 classes, instructors must have a current group fitness certification from a nationally recognized organization such as ACE, AFAA, NDEITA, or ACSM. They must also have a current CPR certification. They can then attend the intensive 2-day Fit For 2 Instructor Training Program and, after completion, teach at a licensed Fit For 2 facility.

Any Start-up costs?

To license the Fit For 2 program, there is an initial fee of $500.00, which includes training for up to 2 instructors. Additional instructors may attend the training for a fee of $199.00 each. The monthly license fee is based on average class attendance and ranges from $50.00 to $200.00.

If an individual is licensing Fit For 2, she may have additional start-up costs such as rental of a facility, equipment purchase, and liability insurance. If she decides to purchase advertising in her local media outlets, she would have that expense as well.

What are your rates?

Same as above.

What services do you offer?

For our licensees, we provide excellent marketing and PR support. Each licensee receives a template for class fliers that can be personalized to each location. They also receive a press release prepared by our corporate office to send to their local media outlets announcing the opening of Fit For 2 classes in their community. The Fit For 2 website (**www.fitfor2.com**) has a page devoted to class locations with pricing information and driving directions. Because Fit For 2 and its owner, Lisa Stone, are featured regularly in the national media, licensees receive exposure for their local programs as well.

We also provide all necessary release forms and articles so that our licensees are legally protected. Each licensee receives a phone script to use when fielding telephone calls from potential class members so that accurate information is always at the front desk person's fingertips.

For our certified Fit For 2 instructors, we provide access to our password-protected online message board so that instructors can share choreography tips, marketing ideas, and job openings. Instructors are kept up to date on the latest research via electronic communications from our corporate office.

How do you market your business?

Locally, we market the Fit For 2 classes primarily through the distribution of fliers and posters to local ob/gyn offices, pediatric offices, maternity stores, and baby furniture stores. Periodically, we advertise in the local parenting magazine, but we haven't found that to be the most effective means of getting new clients into our classes. We've also exhibited at area baby expos, but, again, haven't found that to be very effective either. Really, the most common way that new clients find our classes is through a friend who has attended Fit For 2. Word of mouth is worth its weight in gold!

Nationally, we market the Fit For 2 program mainly through our website and through media write-ups. Our listing in the Entrepreneur Magazine Small Business Opportunities issue garners tremendous interest in our program, both in the US and in Mexico.

Overall, though, our most effective means of marketing is through Lisa Stone's interviews in the local and national media. Our corporate office regularly sends out press releases on topics of current interest in hopes of securing media exposure. Ms. Stone has appeared on NBC's Today Show, CNN Headline News, CNN Parenting Today, CNN Health News, and in Fit Pregnancy Magazine, Fitness Magazine, ePregnancy Magazine, Pregnancy Magazine, and Weight Watchers Magazine, among others.

Will you ever expand?

We are continually looking for additional licensees for Fit For 2 so that communities everywhere have a quality fitness program to offer pregnant women and new mothers. With the growing epidemic of obesity in the US, especially among children, it becomes crucial for parents to be positive role models for their families by participating in regular physical activity. Fit For 2 is a way for mothers to teach their children about the benefits of being active, even before they're born!

Do you have any tips for other mothers?

Fit For 2 is a wonderful business for mothers who want to be available for their children during the day. The key is to set aside specific space for your business and specific working hours, though those hours may vary day to day. Also, if your office will be in your house, it is very helpful to set up a separate phone line for your business that you can answer only during business hours—a voicemail system is essential to answer after-hours calls.

How do you balance your kids and business?

Balancing kids and business is a challenge for all moms who work outside the home. There are many days that the pendulum swings too far to one side or the other, so the challenge then becomes finding an overall weekly or monthly balance instead of a daily one. When school is in session, I try to limit my business time so that I'm finished when the school bus arrives. During school breaks, it becomes a bit more challenging to separate work and family time. Now that my children are older, they are more understanding when I tell them I have to work, but when they were younger I found that I needed to keep activities for them in my office.

How about your spouse?

Since my spouse is an attorney and works very long hours, working him into the equation really isn't much of a problem. He's usually home later in the evenings after I've completed my work for the day. The challenge usually comes when we both need time to work on the weekend. It's at those times that we resort to hiring someone to stay with our children so we can both do what we need to do. Sometimes, we end up keeping the sitter into the evening so the two of us can have a quiet dinner together, alone!

What is your biggest challenge?

My biggest challenge is keeping up with all the requests for information that I receive via the Internet and making sure to follow up with them on a timely basis. My strength lies in my creativity and teaching skills, and I struggle a bit with the sales aspect of Fit For 2. I would like to find someone to work with me and handle the marketing and licensing of Fit For 2 so I'm free to develop more class formats and produce additional video workouts.

Any rewards for doing this?

I am a baby fiend! Getting to hold babies every day in my classes is a huge reward for me and prevents me from over-populating the world on my own! The entire pregnancy/birth process fascinates me, so I love being surrounded by women going through it every day. When my pregnant clients come back to class after having their babies, they always tell me how much being fit helped them cope with labor and delivery—that brings a huge smile to my face!

Any other advice for mothers?

If you are going to start a home-based business, make sure it's something about which you are passionate. There are many obstacles involved in running a business and a family at the same time so if you don't love what you're doing, it's going to be tough. Also, make sure your family and close friends are supportive of your decision to start a business—you may need to call on them for last-minute childcare!

Lisa's contact information:

Lisa Stone, President
Fit For 2, Inc.
http://www.fitfor2.com
Phone: 770.509.8078
Fax: 770.509.0668
Email: **lisa@fitfor2.com**

Potty training sticker books and handmade ornaments

Name: Tracy Foote
Business: TracyTrends
Website: **www.TracyTrends.com**

In Tracy's business, she owns a novelty gift shop specializing in potty training sticker books and handmade remembrance ornaments.

Why did Tracy start her business?

I began the business to bring in a little money while raising my children at home as well as to have some fun with my hobbies.

I began over in England when the Teletubbie craze was brand new. I realized I had access to products that one could not get in the USA. Slowly, I learned the rules of eBay and how selling could work on the Internet.

Back in the states, I was toying with computer graphics and scanning images of my children (while trying to toilet train my son) when I had the idea of a toilet training activity book. Why should they color TV characters when they could be focusing on the task at hand?

So I auctioned off my china (which was gathering dust anyway as entertaining went out the door with child number one). I bought my own binding machine and designed printed and bound my own books at home. I am going to a national printer and hope that time I spent binding can now be spent marketing and getting even more books in children's hands. Plus I have added 2 new books, My Potty Reward Stickers for Boys/Girls: 126 Stickers and Chart to Motivate Toilet Training.

Are there any requirements for this kind of business?

I am a self-taught Internet person, so there are no qualifications except the desire, commitment and having the time to learn.

Any Start-up costs?

I began selling on eBay so initially there were no start up costs. Later as sales grew, I began my own website with a free host and then later expanded to a paid host with a merchant account. I truly financed my company through auctioning off children's clothes and items we rarely used around the house.

What are your rates?

The rates vary.

What services do you offer?

TracyTrends.com focuses on Internet retail sales and free promotional swaps with other companies of similar target audiences.

How do you market your business?

I truly believe some of my marketing success is in Keywords. I learned that people search by keywords.

I am very careful when describing my products to choose words people would actually type in. In eBay auctions, I was NOT selling My Potty Activity Book +45 Toilet Training Tips: Parent/Child Interaction with Coloring and Creative Fun. First that would be too long. Second, no one will type that in. No, I was selling: Potty Training BK +45 Toilet Tips. That is my auction title because the buyer will be typing Toilet training, potty training, tip etc. TracyTrends.com also markets through word of mouth and through sharing advertising flyer with other moms. I hand out some of theirs and they hand out some of mine. I have tried a few newspapers and I watch for any opportunities to advertise for FREE.

Will you ever expand?

Yes, I would like to someday have a real storefront.

Do you have any tips for other mothers?

Go slow and try to spend nothing until you have brought in something to spend. If it's FREE, it's for me!

How do you balance your kids and your business?

I believe one must have set hours and stick to them. I also watch for any spare moment I have. If I am on a long car ride, waiting for a swim class to end, etc. I bring something work related to do.

How about your spouse?

Well, he still calls it, "Tracy's Hobby Business" so we are working on that. However, he was excited when someone placed my Too Close To Call Christmas ornament in Time Magazine, Dec. 4, 2000. And he is always there to help with computer crashes (smile).

What is your biggest challenge?

The biggest challenge will be setting limits and goals because I want to do it all. You need limits in how much time you will spend on business, spouse, children and friends. I must re-look at my priority list every few days while thinking long and short-term goals.

Any rewards for doing this?

I feel reward for every satisfied customer and when I am able to help other moms promote as in the swapping of information. The greatest reward though is inspiring your children. I am home to be with them so every accomplishment of theirs makes me proud. If a little of my example runs off on them, all the better. I was very proud of my six-year-old who brought me her first book; "The Tiniest Lunch" stapled with jagged edge pages. If I don't make the best seller list, maybe she will!

Any other advice for mothers?

The time to stop is when you are no longer having fun!

Tracy's contact information:

Tracy Foote, Director TracyTrends.com
Author of:
My Potty Activity Book +45 Toilet Training Tips
(ISBN:0-615-11462-8; 097082260X)
My Potty Reward Stickers for Boys and Girls
(ISBN:0-9708226-2-6 & 0-9708226-1-8)
2084 Briarwood Street
Prattville, AL 36066 USA
Voice:208-575-4350-1
Fax:208-575-4350-2

HERBAL PRODUCTS

Name: Melissa Roberts
Business: Roo's Garden
Website: **http://www.roosgarden.com**

In Melissa's business, she makes all natural herbal soaps, bath and beauty products using only natural oils and essential oils.

Why did Melissa start her business?

Roo's Garden was founded on the belief that we should emphasize our connections with nature, and bring the wonders of the garden more fully into our lives.

Below is part of our Mission Statement:

Gardening has always been an enjoyable pastime for us. When our daughter ("Roo") was born it became even more important. Our herbs and flowers were a means of teaching our daughter about or connection and responsibility to the rest of nature. Motivated by her love of eating our fresh herbs, Roo quickly caught the family passion for gardening. She claimed our plants as her own, hence "Roo's Garden".

In an effort to care for and teach our children, we have applied ourselves to discovering the many properties and virtues of the plants we grow. As we grow with her, we have learned more ways to being the essence of her garden into the home.

Are there any requirements for this kind of business?

The requirements involve knowledge and love of herbs and their many virtues, as well as an understanding of the best ways to make these properties available for use. This includes an understanding of the many materials and processes for making the soaps, balms, lotions and other herbal products. For example, many oils may be used to produce soap. However, each has a different chemical makeup. These must be appreciated to obtain a final product that will meet your needs... Creativity is also in high demand in our business. Designing the scents, names, colors, packaging, promotional materials, etc., all draw extensively from the creative pool. Additionally, a commitment to the goal of building and maintaining a *business* is a necessity. This requires hours of paper work, promotion, researching, cost efficiency monitoring, etc. All of which are requirements, and all are work. In this business, it also means accepting that you will not get rich quickly, if at all!

Any Start-up costs?

We have tried to keep our start up costs at a bare minimum. In the first ½ of the first year I only bought enough to see me through a few orders. For my type of business and the fact that I only sell via Internet—it was an absolute must for me to have an up to date computer. I am also a programmer and knew that I would be doing web design and programming. I needed a computer that would accommodate the software I needed. There were also costs for other materials:

- Paper goods for business cards, invoices, fliers, labels

- Boxes for packaging, and mailing

- Mailing supplies such as tape, peanuts

- Pens, computer ink, new printer/copier

- Packing material such as organza bags, ribbon, baskets, Spanish Moss

- Essential oils, bath salt supplies, raw materials for soap.

- Internet connection, domain registration, hosting fees

- Insurance, membership fees, business license

What are your rates?

Rates for our products range from $4.00 to $50.00 depending on what you are ordering. Our herbal soaps are approximately 4oz each and are $4.00 per bar. Our gift baskets range from $20.00 to $50.00 depending on size.

What services do you offer?

Roo's Garden is a small home base company, providing bath and beauty products for both retail and wholesale accounts. For wholesale customers I offer all products with our label, Private Label (meaning your company logo/name on our products), or 'naked' (where you label on your end). For Private Label I am happy to help with packaging design and/or logo creation.

How do you market your business?

I market my business via word of mouth, submit to search engines, links. I also participate in various media blitz that are offered to members of the Handmade Toiletries Network (of which I am a member).

Will you ever expand?

Growth management remains a major concern for our business. While the opportunity to expand is exciting, it raises many issues. In terms of time commitment (which equals time reduction in other aspects of life), the array of issues that arise when hiring staff, etc. Presently, we prefer to maintain a business size in keeping with the needs of our family, and that does not exceed our abilities to self-produce our products and maintain our personal involvement with our clients (including personalizing orders if desired).

Do you have any tips for other mothers?

Starting and maintaining your own business is extremely rewarding but it is also a tremendous amount of work. Having the support of family is crucial! With my type of business you have to help, someone to watch your children while you are creating the soap (this is not something you do with children in the room). Above all believe in your self and what you are creating. Research and more research before you start your business so that you know what you are getting into. Know all the ins and outs of the type of business you want to start. Join an organization of like individuals who can give you further support.

How do you balance your kids and your business?

That is one of the hardest things that I face with this business. Much of my work is done at night after my children are tucked into bed. Luckily my spouse will stay close to the children while they are falling asleep in case they need anything so that I can safely and without interruption complete some work. There are times when work is put on hold for the needs of my children—they will always come first. When that happens I will work late the next night to catch up or I will ask that my spouse step in and help me package orders.

I also involve my children as much as possible. Our daughter helps us to pick out the names for our products. She mostly works with the children's products and has recently named 3 children's Monster Away NightTime sprays. Our son is our "sniffer" and after I create a new scent we ask him if he likes it, a huge "YUM" means it is a keeper.

How about your spouse?

My situation appears to be rather unique in that my husband is also part owner of Roo's Garden. This is a joint venture and he supports me in all things related to the business, even the sometimes incredibly long work nights! My spouse creates all the designs for our products. He also creates the colors for the soaps and helps me with the scents. He is also great at helping with my two young children on nights when I absolutely have to get some work done. I can honestly say that without my spouse this business would not exist. Roo's Garden is truly a family business.

What is your biggest challenge?

Remembering that just because I am a Type A personality that I do need to sit back and relax and spend good quality time with my family. That this business is truly for our joy and that as long as we are happy that is what counts. I don't have to explore every avenue of marketing, I don't have to accept every order, I don't have to create all these fabulous products that are running through my mind. I don't have to do any of this if it is keeping me from enjoying the creation of my products and the fun of my family.

Any rewards for doing this?

Knowing that others like what I create! It is thrilling to know that my products can be found not only in the US but Internationally. That people find me through word of mouth and they to love my products. The biggest reward is showing others all the wonderful products that can be created from using what nature gives.

Any other advice for mothers?

If you have a love, talent and desire to start your own business then go for it! Constantly re-evaluate where you are and where you want to be with your business. Are you there? Have you exceeded what you wanted to do and need to pull back? What do you need to do to achieve your goals?

Melissa's contact information:

Roo's Garden

http://www.roosgarden.com

All natural herbal soaps, bath and beauty products using only natural oils and essential oils.

Enjoy the textures, scents, colors and allure of fine herbal products from Roo's Garden. Selling both retail and wholesale.

RESIDENTIAL DESIGNER

Name: Dawn Vaughan
Business: VHDesign—custom and stock house plans
Website: **http://www.vhdesign.com**

In Dawn's business, she works out of her home office as a Residential Designer.

Why did Dawn start her business?

I began working for an architectural firm during college, then went on to work full-time as a draftsperson at Stennis Space Center, doing house plans at night. But I always knew that I wanted to be able to stay home and raise my children once we had our family, if I could just find a way to work at the same time. I finally quit my job in 1987. The children followed shortly. Jordan in 1989, Chelsea in 1991, and Savannah in 1996. I began my business slowly, doing 5-6 plans a year. Back then all our work was done hunched over a drafting table, but now we have computer software that keeps us hunched over our keyboard. We've also made the commitment to homeschool, so that's another challenge that I've been able to meet and still continue to have my business grow. The last two years have been the toughest to manage, as I developed an ongoing illness, which required six surgeries in a year's time. The illness is now under control with medication and things are starting to get back to normal.

Are there any requirements for this kind of business?

I spent two years in high school in the vocational program for drafting and design, then two years at a Community College earning my associate's degree in Drafting and Design. I have twenty years' experience designing and drafting just about every kind of residential and light commercial structure you can imagine. I've done everything from a small one-bedroom home cabin, a 10,000 square foot mansion, apartments, and even several fire stations! Presently, I am studying for the certification exam to become a Certified Professional Building Designer, which I will need to have my designs published in national magazines. The exam is two days, 21 hours and covers all aspects of building design—engineering, structural calculations, architectural history, and actual manual (on a drafting board) design and drafting of a set of house plans.

Any Start-up costs?

My start-up costs were minimal. When I first began, all I needed was a drafting board, paper and drafting supplies (triangles, T-square, mechanical pencils, scales, etc.). I later was given the computer and then bought the software, and out-source the plotting and blueprinting. Eventually, I acquired my own plotter and blueprint machine. We now have 5 computers, 3 printers, a plotter, blueprint machine, 5 desks, bookcases, filing cabinets, and assorted chairs in my remodeled garage home office. All in all, after fifteen years, I have invested probably $40,000 in equipment and remodeling costs for my business, but it was all done very slowly.

What are your rates?

Typical rates for architect's services run anywhere from $5 per square foot to 20% of the actual construction costs of the home. A Residential Designer charges much less while providing nearly the same services. I have 3 different packages I offer my clients, which run from 40c—75c per square foot, or $36 an hour. Once I become a CPBD (Certified Professional Building Designer) I will be able to charge much higher rates for essentially the same service I now provide.

What services do you provide?

I do total design and drafting services for the client. I receive their sketches, photographs, and survey of property—basically anything they can give me to convey their ideas to me, then use those to design a 3D model of the home. I then create graphics from that 3D model and upload those to the client's webpage for them to view. They tell me what changes they need, I change the 3D model, create new graphics and upload them, and the process continues until the client is totally satisfied. A sample of this page can be seen at **http://www. vhdesign.com/whiley.htm.**

Then the construction drawings are completed and the finished blueprints are shipped to the client. This process allows me to work with anyone in the country, or even internationally. I've worked with several clients outside of the United States. It's simply a matter of finding out the building code used in their area, and designing to that code.

How do you market your business?

I used to spend money on local yellow page ad and newspaper ads, but now that all the local builders know me, I no longer do that. I depend solely on word of mouth or builders for local work. On the Internet, I advertise mostly on pay-per-click specialty directories for my field, such as my own directory at **http://www.homedesign-directory.com**, or at pay-per-click engines such as overture or google for the keywords "house plan" or "home plan". I also advertise my website sweepstakes, in which we give away a free custom house plan, as well as several stock plans and lesser prizes. I participate as much as I can in **http:// themompack.com**, which is a co-op of moms who work at home. We send out "mompacks" in our orders, which contain fliers, coupons, business cards, samples, etc. from other moms in our group. Donating prizes to other's contests is also a great way of advertising my business and I usually donate at least one set of plans each month.

Will you ever expand?

There have been many times in the last year, when I was either working 18-hour days or in the bed after another surgery trying to design with a laptop, that the thought of hiring designers to help me was very tempting! I do have some temporary outside help, in the form of designers who work with my software and live in other states. They take on some of my workload when I get overwhelmed. I'm not sure that I would ever expand into an office "in town" with a big staff, at least until the children are grown and on their own.

Do you have any tips for other mothers?

Don't make the same mistake I did, and always put the business ahead of the family. I've done that far too often, but am now trying to remedy that and try to keep to a set work schedule. Like time to just "hang out" with the kids when they want to play, or watch a movie with hubby when he wants some alone time with me. But, yet enough time for me to get my work done, as well as study for my upcoming exam. After all, the whole reason I became a work-at-home mom was to be home for my family! The only downfall with the Internet, that I've found, is that most people see your webpage and expect you to be "at work", no matter what time of the day or night it is. They could be on the other side of the world, but they forget that there are time zones, and that people do not work 24 hours a day.

How do you balance your kids and your business?

Balancing my kids and the business is probably the hardest part of being a work-at-home mom, especially since we homeschool. We have to be very flexible in everything we do. Some nights I may stay up all night working on a house for a deadline, then have to do the home-schooling, then meet with clients all afternoon and all evening, then work some more. When the kids were younger, I had a "mother's helper", a teenager who came in everyday after school, and all day during the summers, to help me with the kids when I had a meeting with a client, or needed to run an errand. These days, the older two kids are 11 and 12, so they are able to entertain the six-year-old when I have a client meeting. Jordan even has a job running blueprints for me, and makes an impressive allowance for a pre-teen! I've been showing him basic home design and he's now planning on becoming an architect when he's grown up and joining me in what would become the "family" business.

How about your spouse?

Ronnie is fantastic. He's the one who encouraged me to learn CAD and wean myself from the drafting board when I was so set in my ways. He then encouraged me to learn HTML and create my first website back in 1995. He's a computer programmer and maintains the computer network in our office, as well as being the resident "computer consultant" for all my endless questions. He never complains, even when he has to come in after a full day of work and "take up the slack" with grocery shopping, cooking or cleaning. We work as a team, which is an absolute must for a work-at-home business.

What is your biggest challenge?

My biggest challenge is time management. Everyone wants (and needs) a piece of my time each day, and the goal is to keep everyone happy while keeping my sanity! I recently hired a virtual assistant, Nancy Brown of **www.virtualgalfriday.net**, who is amazing. She is taking on the job of my bookkeeping, which is a mess, as I never have time to handle it, and keeping up with my mailing list. As we get more organized, she will take over more and more of the jobs that I can delegate to her, which will free me up to spend more time on designing. I am even planning an e-book catalog of all my designs, which she will eventually help me with as well. Hiring Nancy, as well as working out our new schedule, has helped tremendously. I even carry a small laminated copy of my schedule in my purse. So, when someone asks me to volunteer for some position, instead of my usual answer; "Yes, of course." I now ask them to look at the schedule and tell me where I can carve the time out without sacrificing homeschooling, work time, study time, sleep time, devotion time, housework, and so on. If they can do that, then I'm all theirs.

Any rewards for doing this?

My lifestyle may be crazy to most people, but the rewards are many. My children are growing up to be mature, responsible, caring people, who see how hard we work to have what we have, and hopefully, appreciate it all the more. I'm here to hug them or lend an ear when they need to talk over some problem, read or play with them (almost) when the mood strikes, and take family vacations when it's cheapest and least crowded during the regular school year. We can take off from work and school on a beautiful sunny day when I'm not very busy, and go to the beach or the park or the zoo. I may never have a spotless house or dinner on the table at 6 p.m. every night, or an exciting social calendar, but those are sacrifices we're willing to make to reap the rewards of a happy family and the satisfaction of a career for me.

Any other advice for mothers?

Don't let your business take over your life. I recently asked each of my kids to answer some questions for me:

What is the best thing about Mom working at home? What is the worst thing about Mom working at home? And, *What would you change if you could?* Each one answered basically the same—that I'm home all day with them. (Savannah added, "to do school with me") The worst part is that I work too much, and the thing they would change is that I would work less so they could spend more time with me! That really opened my eyes and was the driving force behind hiring Nancy and working out the schedule that we have now. I was letting the business consume my life, thinking that the more I worked, the better our lives would be. I was never so wrong! I can theoretically have my business for years to come, but my kids are only here with me for a short time. I want to use those years as wisely as I possibly can.

Dawn's contact information:

Dawn M. Vaughan
Summer Sweepstakes—$1200+ in prizes!

Grand Prize: $500 custom-designed house plan!
http://www.vhdesign.com
VHDesign—custom and stock house plans

PHOTOGRAPHIC MEMORIES

Name: Lori Betz
Business: Mother's Day Out!
Website: **http://www.mothersdayout.com**

In Lori's business, she provides quality products that are customized with a photo, text and/or logo for families and businesses.

Why did Lori start her business?

When my second son was born and with some serious health problems, I gave up my part-time job and became a full time Mother. In 1997, my third son was born. With 3 children, I certainly didn't need another job on top of being a full time Mother. However, I started to get the "itch" to do something else. I have a bachelor's degree in Journalism/Public Relations, so I really wanted to do something in that area. I live in a rural area of Colorado, so the "career' options in Journalism are, well, zilch. This is especially true for part-time. I found the Internet interesting, so I created Mother's Day Out! (**http://www.mothersdayout.com**) in 03-98. Photographic Memories by Mother's Day Out! (**http://www.mothersdayout.com/mdomall.htm**) was created about 6 months later. I really enjoy working on the site and filling orders from Photographic Memories. It lets me use my creative mind, and still be home with my 3 children.

Are there any requirements for this kind of business?

You must be creative and work well with a computer. You can start with only a basic knowledge of a computer, but you will need to learn to work with computer design programs and graphics. Many programs are very easy to learn.

Any Start-up Costs? The basic essentials to start a printing business are:

1. A computer that is able to run the latest programs and work well with graphics.

2. A quality printer that does well with photos and graphics. $200 and up.

3. A program that will design the products you need such as stationery, cards and etc. These start at $25.00 and go up.

4. Other products such as paper, postage and etc. can be purchased as you receive orders if your budget is very tight.

What are your rates?

My products range from $3.00 and go up. Shipping is low and orders over $50.00 have free shipping.

What services do you provide?

I provide quality products that can be customized with a photo, text and/or logo for families and businesses. Some of my products include stationery, greeting cards, webcards, recipe cards, mousepads, shirts, bookmarks, coasters, night lights, watches and many more.

How do you market your business?

I advertise on other sites that target families and home business owners. I purchase advertising and swap advertising with other sites and newsletters. I also submit my site to search engines, direct mail, free sample offers and more. I also belong to some online organizations that help promote businesses.

Will you ever expand?

I don't have plans for expansion at this point. I am very busy with the products I have.

Do you have any tips for other mothers?

Do your research. Be sure it will be something you love. Starting a home business requires patience and lots of work. It is less stressful if you don't need a specific income from your business in the beginning. This will allow you to work on your business when you have the time. Stay away from the get rich quick schemes. All businesses require some type of start up fee, but be careful. Make sure you know the company such as Tupperware or etc. It isn't safe to send money to someone you know nothing about. Check out the Better Business Bureau.

How do you balance your kids and your business?

I try to work when my kids are at school or in bed. It's harder with very young children. If you have children who aren't in school or in pre-school, you may want to consider hiring a baby-sitter for a few hours or join a *Mother's Day Out!* program. Many times these programs will require some time from you, but won't cost you anything to have childcare for your children.

How about your spouse?

Fortunately, I can work when he is at work also. If I need to work in the evenings, he is often home to take care of the kids while I work.

What is your biggest challenge?

My biggest challenge is finding enough time to work. My business requires selling my product to others and obtaining new customers. It's hard to find time for marketing and business promotion.

Any rewards for doing this?

My business allows me to help other Mothers and to be creative. I love designing products for people. My best rewards are when customers let me know how much they love my products.

Any other advice for mothers?

Advertising is expensive. Again, research your advertising options. Many times you can barter your products for advertising at another site, exchange or swap advertising and etc. When you advertise, be sure to track it. You will need to know which ads are bringing you business and which ones aren't. Many times it takes a while for the ad to work. Don't expect huge results in a short time.

Lori's contact information:

Mother's Day Out!
http://www.mothersdayout.com
Photographic Memories by Mother's Day Out!
http://www.mothersdayout.com/mdomall.htm
Email contact: mdo@montrose.net
Address: P.O. Box 654
Montrose, Co. 81402-0654

FREELANCE WRITER

Name: Tina L. Miller of Merrill, Wisconsin
Business, Co-owner & Editor in Chief of Obadiah Press and Obadiah
Magazine, Author of "When A Woman Prays."
Website: **www.tinalmiller.com** and **www.obadiahpress.com**

Tina is a freelance writer and editor of a magazine and motivational
speaker.

Why did Tina start her business?

In September 1999 I was downsized from my job as a supervisor/team
development facilitator—along with 1,000 others—at a large insurance company. While losing my job came as a shock, it turned out to
be a blessing in disguise. I had been diagnosed with Multiple Sclerosis
less than a year before and really wanted to pursue my dream to be a
writer full-time rather than trying to fit it in around everything else.
(The MS diagnosis made me realize life is too short to wait for "someday" to follow your dreams—and at times it limited my energy level,
making it difficult to work full-time *and* write part-time.) This provided the perfect opportunity to launch my writing career full-time,
and I've been writing ever since. Mind you, I wasn't generating much
income (if any) for a good long time. It takes a while to get established
in this business, to get clips with reputable publications, get assign-
ments from good-paying publications, and establish a number of
repeat clients. But I really enjoy what I'm doing, so the payoff is more
than monetary—my job satisfaction is very high! Sometimes that's
more important. In October 2000 I met my partner, LaDonna
Meredith, online and we immediately hit it off. We became business
partners and launched Obadiah Press and Obadiah Magazine within
just a few short months, and by January 2001, we had our first issue of
Obadiah Magazine in subscribers' hands. In January 2002 we had our
first two books in print under our Obadiah Press imprint, one of which
was my first published book, "When A Woman Prays."

We're releasing our next book entitled "911: The Day America Cried—A collection of poems, letters, and stories on an American tragedy," which contains the writings of more than 80 authors from all around the country and is compiled by Victoria Walker, the first week in September. And we just got a distributor to get all our books into bookstores. To say that I've been working night and day, 24/7, for the last three years is probably an understatement. But I love what I do. Today I am busier than I have ever been, I'm almost to the point of having to turn some work away, and my services are in high demand. I've established a number of regular, very loyal clients and publications that assign me stories regularly. But, of course, I'm still not exactly where I want to be. I guess I climb one mountain, see another in the distance, and set off to conquer that one, too!

I should clarify that I am not making a great deal of money at this point in my writing business despite having more than enough work to fill every hour of my day. Our magazine and publishing house are a long-term venture, one I don't recommend anyone jump into without a lot of pre-planning. Publishing a magazine and books requires my partner and I to contribute money out of our own pocket every month. So we're not at a break even point yet—and from what I've heard about starting any new business, we're looking at a good five years in business before we can expect to. So that is a huge financial challenge! And it's also a time challenge—because I need to focus on my paying writing gigs to help me finance the bigger venture, which will hopefully generate a long-term payoff for us.

Are there any requirements for this kind of business?

Having cautioned your readers against actually starting their own magazine and publishing house without a ready supply of cash, I can say that starting work as a freelance writer is a whole lot easier. If you have a gift for writing, I'd suggest you "go for it" with that! Becoming a freelance writer is something you can even do in your spare time or on a part-time basis until it begins to generate more income for you.

The requirements of being a freelance writer and/or editor? You have to have a firm grasp on the language. For me, of course, that means English, Grammar, spelling, punctuation, sentence structure, and how to write. You need to be a good writer. There is no substitute for good writing. Having said that, you also need guts, patience, and persistence. Writing is not so much about writing as it is rewriting, rewriting, rewriting, and rewriting some more. Writers don't just sit down and whip out a first draft and send it in. We spend a lot of time polishing, editing, tweaking, and perfecting our prose—or ad copy or web content or whatever it is you're writing—until is absolutely shines. That's what we're hired to do. We're communication experts. And that expertise has to come shining through. The guts, patience, and persistence come in because it's a rare writer who gets their first submission accepted or lands a client right away. You will need to do what every writer does when you're just getting started: write, send it in, and wait. You will get rejections—because even the best writers do and that's just part of paying your dues in this business. You'll have to wait around for answers a lot, so it's a good idea to just write something else and send it to another publication instead of driving yourself crazy. But if you study the markets, apply for writing jobs, get your name out there, and keep writing and sending your stuff out there, there's a good chance it will pay off.

It's also important to have some backup or supplementary income (or keep your day job) until your writing career begins to pay off—and if you're married, a spouse who is at least minimally supportive is a must. Hubbies tend to get cranky when they think you're going to be bringing in income at your at-home job and they discover that there are some pretty lean months in the writing business, especially before you get your business established. I know writers who have very supportive spouses and others who don't. It's a lot easier for the ones who do.

Any Start-up costs?

For a writer, start up costs seem rather minimal—at least as compared to many other business ventures since you don't have to rent office or retail space or pay for inventory—(unless you decide to self-publish).

The absolute basics I recommend in this day and age are:

- A good PC with a CD-ROM and floppy drive and a CD writer and lots of memory. Make sure it's a reliable machine because you're going to use it a LOT!

- Internet access and a business email account.

- Telephone access—and if you're using one line for your phone calls and Internet access, use an Internet answering service or get a second phone line. If you can afford it, opt for cable modem or a second phone line so that you can be online and on the phone simultaneously.

- A good printer/photocopier/fax. I really like the all-in-one units.

- Basic office supplies like paper, pens, ink cartridges, file folders, staples and stapler, scissors and tape, a calculator, etc. Stuff you probably already have around anyway.

- A desk and a good desk chair. You're going to spend a lot of time in that chair, so make sure it's comfortable. You can get by with a card table and a folding chair for a while if you have to.

- Writing reference books: a dictionary (an absolute must!), an annual Writers Market guide, a good English/grammar/punctuation book for reference; possibly a style manual.

- If you can afford it, file cabinets and bookshelves will come in handy.

- Also, a membership in a book club like Writers Digest Book Club and the money to invest in your "education" reading or taking writing classes is a very good investment.

What are your rates?

Rates are hard to provide. As a writer, I sometimes charge by the word; other times I charge by the hour; and still other times I charge by the project. There are a lot of different factors that go into it. When you're just starting out, ANY paying job is a good writing job. It helps you get clips and prove yourself. These days I won't take just any job. But I will sometimes take a lower paying job if it has other perks:

a. I like the subject matter and enjoy doing it.

b. It's a long-term client I really like.

c. It will provide me with regular assignments/regular work.

d. There are other benefits like publicity for my book and the magazine or some other intangible perk. There are a few rare occasions where I've even bartered for services.

What services do you provide?

Right now I do a lot of different things—and the variety is nice because it keeps things interesting—but it's also really hard to keep up with. (I sometimes feel pulled in all different directions and would actually recommend new writers focus their efforts a little more than I have to avoid the extra challenges and stress this presents!) I write, of course. That includes writing for magazines, newspapers, online ezines, and trade publications, my own magazine, and my books. I have other books that will be published in the next year or so. I also write for my individual and corporate clients—and for them, I've written everything from ad copy to web site content, newsletters, articles, proposals and business correspondence, workbooks, leader and teleclass guides, and more. I edited seven books over the last two years, and I teach online writing classes. (See my website for information on how you can become a writer, too!) I do complete newsletter, book, and magazine layouts—both for Obadiah and for clients—and that basically includes everything from editing to creating the final file that will go directly to the printer. I create basic web sites for clients on occasion and will maintain their site and provide content updates. I also provide total project management services for one client—a not-for-profit organization—handling telephone calls and contacts, maintaining organizational records, writing their correspondence, attending meetings and preparing minutes, handling financials, doing their newsletter, and more. Of course, I also edit Obadiah Magazine. And when time allows, I still enjoy the opportunity to speak at conferences or conduct motivational seminars. Somewhere in there I manage to fit in some promotional efforts for my book, lead a writer's group once a month, and mentor other writers.

How do you market your business?

My website has been instrumental in helping me establish my business—both from the standpoint of helping potential clients find me and also in defining myself as a writer, showing potential clients what I can do, and establishing my professional image. I also maintain a current writer's resume and a portfolio of my work—including online links to my work—that I can provide potential markets or clients for review. I share my business cards with people wherever I go and can do so in a professional manner. And I talk about what I do with people in conversation whenever possible. I also actively seek out business. Workings with local agencies to take on some of their overflow work (in fact that is one of the way you can get established). Applying for writing jobs online (you'll get a LOT of rejections before you ever land one, but try not to get discouraged), and querying markets continually.

But probably THE most effective "marketing" is word of mouth. One satisfied client or someone I know will recommend me to someone looking for a writer or editor—then we get together by phone or email to talk—and we just click. A recommendation from someone who knows my work is priceless!

Will you ever expand?

That's a really good question—and one I've been thinking a lot about. Because I am so busy these days, I've considered subcontracting some of my work out. The problem is, I am a perfectionist and a bit of a control freak—and I have a really high standard for my own work. I'm not sure anyone would want to work for me under such conditions! My clients expect a lot from me, and I always deliver, so I'd have to "tweak" everything before I sent it on. So I'm really not sure. For now, it's just something that crosses my mind every now and again when I'm really stressed out.

Do you have any tips for other mothers?

For mothers, or women, or anyone for that matter, I say—figure out what you love to do and build a career around it. If you want to work at home and have your own business, get creative! Think "outside the box" as they say and don't limit yourself with your preconceived ideas. Imagine what you could do if the limitations or obstacles you see that are holding you back WEREN'T there—and sometimes that will give you a great idea of something you can try that you hadn't thought of before. Life is too short to do something you don't enjoy—and if you look hard enough, you'll find a match for you and make it happen. Also, if you're working outside the home now and you want to be at home, take a good hard look at how much you're actually earning AFTER expenses like daycare, commuting, lunches out, business attire, convenient meals, take-out, and potentially higher income taxes, etc. You may not be netting as much as you thought, so maybe you don't have to bring in what you make now to keep your family in the lifestyle you're accustomed to if you didn't have those expenses because you worked from home.

How do you balance your kids and your business?

My children are 10 and almost 13, so it's a little easier for me now. (Though I did own another home-based business I ran successfully when the kids were small, but that's another story.) I try to spend some one-on-one time with the kids when I can, but I must admit that it is a challenge and I need to do this more often. Sometimes I need to just get out of the house and go do something with them so I'm not thinking about all the work piled in my home office and my living room—or I'd NEVER take a break. So I do things with them and I try to sit down and TALK with them without distractions occasionally to really catch up with what's going on with them.

I also teach my kids independence and responsibility. Just because Mom is working at home doesn't mean Mom is the maid, the cook, the chauffeur, etc. And it doesn't mean I'm on vacation even if they have a day off from school. I still have to work because other people are counting on me. My kids are old enough to help with things—from caring for pets to mowing the lawn, loading the dishwasher, cleaning up the kitchen, and helping with laundry. They also both enjoy cooking, so I frequently let them cook—for me, too! There's nothing like a hot meal when you're rushing to meet a tight deadline—served to you by a 10-year-old with a perky smile on her face because she got to make it! What do I care if it's a cheese quesadilla? It fills the tummy, it's actually healthy, and it works for us!

How about your spouse?

My husband is an over-the-road truck driver so my schedule is really flexible. He is sometimes gone for a week or more at a time, and when he is, I work whatever hours suit me. Often that means working until the wee hours of the morning and then sleeping late in the morning. Of course, that doesn't work as well during the school year.

What is your biggest challenge?

I probably have several big challenges actually. In no particular order. They are:

- Time management or making the most effective use of my time.

- Procrastination (which might actually be in there with time management).

- Making myself take time to relax so I don't get too stressed (that's probably in the time management category, too).

The bottom line is, life is flying by fast and there never seem to be enough hours in the day to accomplish all I've set out to do.

Any rewards for doing this?

I love to write, I love to see my name in print, and I love to get emails, cards, and letters from people who read something I wrote and were deeply affected or moved in some way. Sometimes it's a note from someone who read my book and it changed her life or helped bring her closer to God—or someone who read one of my articles in Obadiah Magazine and it just really struck a chord in them. Those are the absolute BEST! Other times it is a note from someone who saw my website or read something I wrote somewhere else and it affected them in some way—or someone who learned a lot in one of my classes—or positive feedback from a client. Those things just make you feel great!

Any other advice for mothers?

When you're picking a career or looking for business opportunities, follow your heart. Remember there is more to life than money and if you're not doing it for the love of doing it, no amount of money is worth it.

Don't be afraid to ask other people who are already doing what you want to do how they did it. Most will be thrilled to answer your questions.

Finally, when you get where you want to be, reach back and pull someone else up along the way. Be a mentor. It feels wonderful!

Tina's contact information:

Tina L. Miller
Author of "When A Woman Prays" by Tina L. Miller, published by Obadiah Press, ISBN 0-9713266-1-4. Order it for just $17.95 (includes S&H)! Call toll-free: 866-536-3167, send an email, or mail your order to 607 N.
Cleveland Street, Merrill, WI 54452. Also available at Amazon.com.
Email: **tina@tinalmiller.com**
Web site: **www.tinalmiller.com**

LANDSCAPING

Name: Janeen Dewispelare
Business: Pyramid Landscape
Website: none at this time

In Janeen's business, she provides lawn maintenance and landscaping.

Why did Janeen start her business?

She and her husband decided that they wanted their own business after working for other landscaping companies. She now is the sole owner of it. Janeen loves nature and her business keeps her physically fit.

Are there any requirements for this kind of business?

Any bigger landscaping company would dispute that we would need at least a degree in horticulture to be able to cut commercial properties. I don't agree with that.

Any Start-up costs?

• A truck—to haul around your equipment

• A small push lawn mower.

• A trimmer.

• Some equipment may be found at garage sales.

What are your rates?

Our rates vary on each job.

What services do you offer?

Mowing, debris removal and trimming.

How do you market your business?

We started out with an advertisement in the paper for small jobs, threw some prices out to the clientele as to what they had paid in the past and off we went. We met landlords through word-of-mouth.

Our biggest break was when we were parked in front of a store and the manager saw our logo on our truck and asked for a bid.

Right now I have no need to market our business. I am set on clients.

Will you ever expand?

We have already expanded to ten stores lots in neighboring cities and may consider moving to the western suburbs of Chicago where the market is less competitive.

Do you have any tips for other mothers?

I would encourage mothers to never give up on their dreams. We are all capable of doing something that doesn't involve housework!

How do you balance your kids and your business?

The kids enjoy what we do. They often come with me on my mowing days and help pick up litter. My oldest is learning how to use the self-propelled mower by practicing on our lawn. They have also taken part in our other businesses, which include parking lot sweeping, house construction and spring and fall house clean up. We also do snow plowing and they both ride with us and like us to think they tell us where to put the snow!

How about your spouse?

Her spouse is thrilled that she has taken over the business on her own and encourages her.

What is your biggest challenge?

Dealing with competition-very high.

Any rewards for doing this?

Rewards are doing something I love and being outdoors and including my children.

Any other advice for mothers?

Find some talent you enjoy doing that makes you happy and full fills your life. It may not seem to be of any consequence to you, but what you can or may bring to someone else's life though your talent and creativity, will be just a uplifting!

Janeen's contact information:

(563) 529-1890

Baby Clothing Sales

Name: Donna Bliss
Business: My Miracle Baby
Website: **www.MyMiracleBaby.com**

In Donna's business, she has an online baby clothes store.

Why did Donna start her business?

I am an out of work New Yorker who lost my job after 20 years as a marketing professional for computer software firms. I also have experience in the healthcare industry.

After I picked myself up and dusted myself off, I decided to do something that I was truly passionate about and apply those 70 hour work weeks in corporate heck (I mean Corporate America) to something that could benefit my family and me. I had a new baby that was conceived through fertility treatments-after having lost 3 babies. I loved everything about baby products. The look, feel, smell-and boy did I love picking out outfits for my Jillian. From that discovery came the concept for My Miracle Baby.com. I ship out about 50-70 orders a week from my basement that has been converted into a warehouse. (Not bad after being in business for only 6 months.) I also work part time for Kraft/Nabisco Foods and do street fairs every other weekend.

I am having a tough time having lost my mom just weeks ago to brutal lung cancer. I am an only child and she was just 57 years old. She was a single parent and lived in our home and I am truly lost. But I do have my miracle baby.

Are there any requirements for this kind of business?

I believe I am having such success because I have applied the business knowledge obtained from working for all those years to my own business. I have a degree which has absolutely nothing to do with business, but I was educated by IBM and I do have an extensive background in marketing and have been able to take everything I know, bring it altogether, and market the heck out of this site. I have people who tell me they see it everywhere! And that's my intention.

Any Start-up costs?

My first purchase was for a small children's clothing lot on Ebay for $495. I now have $40,000 in inventory. I've also invested in a new computer, laser printer, palm pilot, scale, 800#, PO Box and more storage containers and tubs then you could possibly imagine. The people at Kmart duck when they see me coming!

What are your rates?

Our prices vary.

What services do you provide?

My Miracle Baby offers the ultimate selection in children's clothing at 40-70% off retail. People are astounded by the prices I offer. I purchase clearance items, overstocks, last year's inventory as well as brand new products. I mark them up only about 1/2 of what others do and have built a very strong and loyal customer base in a short time frame.

How do you market your business?

I love this part! Because here is where I thrive and this is where my ambition and drive shows. I send out weekly e-blasts, have a monthly Miracle News Newsletter, exchange links with fellow "Mom Packers" Mommy Mailers and Little Did I Know members. I send out press releases, advertise on the inside cover of Tracy Foote's Potty Activity Book as well as in Gretchen McNally's Baby Web Book. I run ads in other newsletters, deliver "mom packs" to local Lamaze centers, pediatrician offices and every one who comes within 50 feet of me! I also give out $5 off coupons to with every order to keep em coming back. My husband works for the LIRR and we put them up on bulletin boards and hand them out at baby showers. I host home parties and give the host $100 for having it. I participate in street fairs and give out mom packs to every one who walks by. I have totes made with my name on them, a tent with custom graphics advertising the site, business cards, key chains and pencils. We advertise in the local parenting guides, sponsor contests, offer gift certificates for sharing "miracle baby" stories and give as much as we can to charity. Our marketing efforts are relentless!

Will you ever expand?

My goal is to outgrow my home (which is happening already) and move my "warehouse" to an industrial park where I can open to the public 3 days a week. This way I can take back my home, do what I do here at the new place and have some retail traffic a few days a week without committing to the grueling schedule of a retail store.

Do you have any tips for other mothers?

Tenacity and attention to detail. Do whatever you can to *not* look so much like a "mom and pop shop"—at least on the Internet. People need to be sure that when they send you their money they will receive quality products in return. They don't want to get that uneasy feeling. Otherwise they'll drive to the mall. And most of all do what you love. If you don't love it, find something you do. I just lost my mom to lung cancer and I will remind you. This is it-this is your life. You can do something you love everyday or *choose* not to. But it *IS* your choice.

How do you balance your kids and your business?

I had to give up something and I picked sleep! Yikes! I had been working out for more than 10 years-running 1/2 marathons and going to the gym. I got possessed by this business and slacked. And I felt it right away. So I make time to run. And I make time to love my daughter.

How about your spouse?

My husband is a little neglected but he'll be okay.

What is your biggest challenge?

Turning off the brain. When you work out of your home you never "leave for the day." My phone rings up till 11pm with customer care calls. It is 12:41a.m. right now and I should have been in bed hours ago. But here I am. Because you must take every available marketing opportunity (including this one) and run with it!

Any rewards for doing this?

I began living life when I lost my job. I wake up everyday and work my tail off but it's still my choice. I wake up and say "What am I going to do today?" and I get to answer the question. I have definitely lost my rhythm and some of my heart with the loss of my mother but I want to do her proud so I just keep at it.

Any other advice for mothers?

When you are raising your children, keep the "NOs" limited to the important things. And proofread everything!

Donna Bliss
My Miracle Baby
www.MyMiracleBaby.com
PO Box 789
Nesconset, NY 11767
1-800-342-2509

7

HOME BUSINESS IDEAS

Still need more ideas? Here are some business ideas I've come across that you can start at home. Some are under $500 to start. Some you can do with just your computer and some involve you working outside of your home. You might find them interesting and you might not even have known some of them existed. Enjoy!

ONLINE BUSINESSES

Want to join the Internet world? Here are some ideas you can run from your computer.

Online Art gallery

Contact Artists in your community and scan photos of their artwork onto your computer. List them in online Auctions or design your own site and sell them yourself. Charge them a percentage of what they make.

Travel Service

What do you know about the world we live in? Have you traveled abroad? If you know about all the hot spots to go to or the best route, hotels, etc. Then start a website about traveling and sell ads to airlines, hotels, luggage companies, etc. Sounds like a fun one!

Online catalog

Contact companies in your area and offer to sell their products. Scan pictures of their products and put together a nice ad for them.

Are you a little Nostalgic?

Everyone collects something. Form a website about collectibles, trade show, old books, auctions, etc.

Teach online!

Are you an expert on some topic? Then teach about it! Start an online class and charge per student.

Become a Webdeveloper

Does everyone always rave over your website? Do you know the difference between Frontpage and the front page of a book? If you are talented enough to design someone else's website, then maybe you should think about going into business for yourself.

How about just the logo?

Logo designing is a hot business and if you know a lot about design, it's worth it. You can charge a lot for this one!

Online PR

Start a business that consists with marketing online businesses. Help publicize their website and related activities. You can do contests and other promotions to lead visitors to their site.

OTHER BUSINESSES...

Make and sell a food item

Are you always being asked to make that special food item or dish? Do you have a flare for cooking? Find out what your local health laws are-you may be able to cook in your own kitchen.

Latch key Program

If you can handle being around lots of kids and have the room for it, open a latchkey after school care out of your home. You would watch kids before or after school until their parents get off work. You might need a van if you don't live near a school. Check to see if you need to be licensed also.

Direct selling

Join a direct selling business. Have home parties and make money and get products free and/or at a discount. Many women make a great living at this type of business. Now a days, you can sell your product online too, which helps a bundle to broaden your customer opportunities.

LIKE ANIMALS?

Try a business that involves those cute and cuddly creatures we adore.

Pet food delivery

Perfect service to sell to seniors or someone who has a house full of pets. Deliver right to their doorstep. Expand to include accessories.

Pet Photography

Do you like to take pictures? You could have fun with this one. Take formal or whimsical pictures of people's pets.

Doggie Daycare

Do you have lots of land? Open a doggie daycare. Let owners run errands while their dog plays at your house.

Pet Products

Buy pet goods at wholesale and sell them to pet owners. This will require a resale license.

Pet matching service

If you like to do research and you like animals, you would like this. You match people to the perfect pet for them. Charge by the hour or figure out a fee.

Customized stuffed animals

If you can sew and have a knack for crafts, try this. A pet owner sends you a photo of their pet and you make a stuffed animal that looks just like it!

How cute!

AND MORE BUSINESS IDEAS...

Errand service

Charge by the hour to run errands for busy people. Shop for presents; pick up laundry, house sit, etc. Check your area for the demand for this.

Gift Baskets

This can be done online and/or through home parties. If you are creative, you will be able to put together lovely baskets for your clients. You might try to be unique and do made-to-order baskets. Which is when, the client tells you what they want to spend and you charge a fee on top it and you put together a basket (using the money they give you) based on what they want to have in it. This way, you have low overhead.

Move—in Cleaning Service

I thought this one was very clever. With the hassles of moving, a person doesn't want to deal with the dirty task of cleaning their new home. So, before they move, in, you come in and get everything ready for them by cleaning rooms, vacuuming, windows, etc. This is different then a maid service in the sense that you will be cleaning empty homes and it's a one time deal with each client-unless you would like to broaden your services into house cleaning. Good way to get clients!

Special effects design

I love stenciling! Do you like to paint and stencil? There are many stencil and faux kits to work with. Many people would like to add these to their rooms but are afraid to try. Check into marbleizing too. They make beautiful results.

Home delivery service

People are very busy these days. The population is getting older and/or busier these days and would like things to come to them. Deliver their prescriptions, groceries, personal items, etc.

BUSINESSES THAT CATER TO KIDS

What about kids? They need services too. This market is growing more then ever. It might be something that your own kids might be able to help with and have fun.

Kids parties

Plan parties for kids. You could either just drop the supplies off or set it up and leave.

Kid proof a home

Great business which you go to the parents homes and childproof it. Are there exposed outlets, sharp corners, and chemicals where they shouldn't be? Do your research on what new products are out there to help make their home a safe haven for their babies.

Treasure Hunt

What fun! Go to the client's house a head of time and map out their treasure hunt. Hide little clues around the house leading to the "treasure chest" at the end.

Dance class

Teach a class on dancing-Pick a type of dance that you are good at or learn a new one. Dance classes are very popular and can be very profitable.

Exercise class

If you don't like to dance, maybe you like to exercise instead? You could teach exercising to parents and their kids. Some states do require licensing.

Teach an art class

If you consider yourself an artist and have the patience to teach others, you can set up a studio in your house and teach children how to paint and draw.

A FINAL NOTE FROM THE AUTHOR

My final advice to all mothers is to do like the tennis shoe ad says and *Just Do It!* Put all your fears aside, take a deep breath and go! Don't look back (well, maybe after your business is doing great, you can look back and say, "Wow!") You have to act on that urge, that feeling in your gut whenever you think about starting that business. You know what that feeling feels like. You feel it-I've felt it. The feeling to succeed, to be home with your children, to watch them grow up and be a part of it. This won't always be an easy path to follow. There will be times that you'll want to cry and give up. But don't fret, there will be more times you'll want to laugh and be glad that you went for it. So, I end with this, I wish you good luck in your adventure and know that no matter what anyone says, you can do it.

ABOUT THE AUTHOR

Teresa Lyons (other than being a mom) is an Author, freelance writer and columnist. She has two wonderful kids (a son and daughter)

Her book, *I'm a Work-at-Home Mommy-You can be too!* was inspired from searching and searching for a reliable work at home source. Wanting to work at home, after time and time again of working long hours at her job, she decided to start a daycare. Curious as to what else was out there and her love of writing, she researched and found out that there were many other moms just like her who wanted to be at home with their children. This inspired her to go after her true dream-writing. She completed her first fiction novel, *The Accident*, by T. A. Lyons in 2002. It is about a woman who is being stalked by someone after her lover is in a terrible accident.

Teresa Lyons has become an expert at giving other moms advice on finding the niche they need to start their own business. Her online magazine, **www.MommysBizatHome.com** is for moms who want to work at home or those who already have a home business. This site also publishes a weekly newsletter to all its members that's full of work-at-home advice, home business ideas, business opportunities and one success story a week.

RESOURCES

Resources for working at home:

Publications

- Small Business Opportunities
  (ISSN 1071-8087)
  Harris Publications, Inc.
  1115 Broadway
  New York, New York 10010

- Home Business Journal.net
  HomeBusinessJournal.net
  9584 Main St.
  Holland Patent, NY 13354

◆   ◆   ◆   ◆   ◆

Clubs or Chapters

- MOMS Club
  c/o 25371 Rye Canyon
  Valencia, CA 91355
  E-mail: **momsclub@aol.com**

- Bizymom Chapter
  www.bizymom.com
  E-mail: **julie@bizymoms.com**

✦   ✦   ✦   ✦   ✦

Other Programs

- The Clairol Mentor Program
  1440 New York Avenue NW, Suite 300
  Washington, DC 20005
  1-212-684-6300

- National Association of Women Business Owners (NAWBO)
  1413 K Street, NW
  Washington, DC 20005
  1-301-608-2590

0-595-25033-5